Additional Pck

"This fantastic memoir is such a welcome change from the glut of motherhood narratives that have been overwhelming bookshelves lately . . . even if you have no interest in parenthood yourself. Mehra and her wife are somehow able to be both pragmatic and idealistic about raising their gender-nonconforming black child as a mixed-race lesbian couple in America." —Sarah Neilson, *BuzzFeed*

"Mehra, a teacher, reflects on her experience as a lesbian daughter of Indian immigrants with an interracial family in this thoughtful memoir-in-essays . . . This insightful, searching book will appeal to anyone contemplating race, family, or growing into oneself."
—*Publishers Weekly* (starred review)

"Mehra's nuanced and thought-provoking work resonates on multiple levels—from the immigrant experience and race relations to accepting one's sexuality, adoption, parenthood, and more. Excellent for readers interested in family and issues of identity in America."
—Gricel Dominguez, *Library Journal* (starred review)

"[Mehra] makes a strong statement about the importance of moving beyond gender and racial barriers toward a more inclusive view of family life. Full of a wide range of insight and emotion, these essays effectively show the difficulties of being a mixed-race, same-sex family in America." —*Kirkus Reviews*

Lauren Schoen

A Note About the Author

NISHTA J. MEHRA was raised among a tight-knit network of Indian immigrants in Memphis, Tennessee. She is the proud graduate of St. Mary's Episcopal School and holds a BA in religious studies from Rice University and an MFA in creative writing from the University of Arizona. An English teacher with more than a decade of experience in middle and high school classrooms, she lives with her wife, Jill, and their child, Shiv, in Phoenix. Connect with her via her website, nishtajmehra.com, and on Twitter and Instagram at @nishtajmehra.

ALSO BY NISHTA J. MEHRA

The Pomegranate King: Essays

Brown
White
Black

Brown
White
Black

An American Family at the Intersection
of Race, Gender, Sexuality, and Religion

Nishta J. Mehra

PICADOR
New York

Picador
120 Broadway, New York 10271

Copyright © 2019 by Nishta J. Mehra
Afterword and Q&A copyright © 2020 by Nishta J. Mehra
All rights reserved
Printed in the United States of America
First published in 2019 by Picador
First Picador paperback edition, 2020

The Library of Congress has cataloged the Picador hardcover edition as follows:
Names: Mehra, Nishta, author.
Title: Brown White Black : an American family at the intersection of race, gender,
    sexuality, and religion / Nishta Mehra.
Description: First edition. | New York : Picador, [2019]
Identifiers: LCCN 2018024338 | ISBN 9781250133557 (hardcover) |
    ISBN 9781250133564 (ebook)
Subjects: LCSH: Mehra, Nishta. | Lesbian mothers—United States—Biography. |
    Racially mixed families—United States—Biography. | Interfaith families—
    United States—Biography. | United States—Race relations.
Classification: LCC HQ75.53 .M44 2019 | DDC 305.800973—dc23
LC record available at https://lccn.loc.gov/2018024338

Picador Paperback ISBN: 978-1-250-29571-2

Designed by Steven Seighman

Our books may be purchased in bulk for promotional, educational, or business
use. Please contact your local bookseller or the Macmillan Corporate and
Premium Sales Department at 1-800-221-7945, extension 5442, or by
e-mail at MacmillanSpecialMarkets@macmillan.com.

Picador® is a U.S. registered trademark and is used by Macmillan Publishing Group, LLC,
under license from Pan Books Limited.

For book club information, please visit facebook.com/picadorbookclub or
e-mail marketing@picadorusa.com.

picadorusa.com • instagram.com/picador
twitter.com/picadorusa • facebook.com/picadorusa

1   3   5   7   9   10   8   6   4   2

The names and identifying characteristics of some persons described in this book have
been changed, as have dates, places, and other details of events in this book.

For Jill and Shiv, my beloveds

Contents

Brown

White

Black

All-American Ethnic Girl

It's a choice each time I stand in front of a Sharpie-wielding barista: "What's the name for the order?" It should be a simple enough question, one that generates an automatic response. Except I always pause. Giving my actual name tends to result in puzzled looks (as if I've somehow said my own name incorrectly), name butchering (everything from "Nisheeta" to "Natasha"), and additional questions (*Where does that come from? What does it mean?*), when all I want is a cappuccino. So I can give my name or I can just make one up and be done with it.

But as tempting as it is to invent a name or use my wife's—Jill—I love my given name too much to pretend that it's something else. I'm one of the few people I know who has always liked her name. Nishta Jaya Mehra. It's assonant, rhythmic, melodic, and, yes, unique: even among Indian kids, there aren't many Nishtas. Because I love my name, I refuse to not use it. I refuse to have it be ignored, to have it go unsaid, to let people call me "Nina" or "whatever you said your name was."

My mom says she first heard the name—traditionally transliterated from Sanskrit as "Nishtha"—as a teenager and decided, *If*

I have a daughter, that will be her name. It translates to something like "dedication" or "intense devotion," which is what it took for my parents to conceive and my mother to successfully carry me to term after three miscarriages and many years of expensive, exhausting fertility treatments. To some, that may feel like a lot of weight to carry, but I don't mind having a name tied to a character trait like dedication. It suits me, though it's hard to say which came first, the name or the temperament. My name also dovetails with the sense of destiny that my mother believed I was fated for. It would seem my name is the origin for my belief in the power of narrative frameworks.

Now that I wear a bindi, people tend to connect me to India right away, but that wasn't always the case. My skin tone lends itself to speculation, like a parlor game people think is fun (not to mention appropriate) to play. I've had a lot of Spanish spoken, presumptively, at me; I don't speak any Spanish. Like many women of color, I've been asked, "Do you work here?" at Gap and the grocery store; I've never worked retail. "Are you his nanny?" white children will ask when seeing me with my son; the brown women they know are nannies and babysitters.

I was born brown in a city divided into black and white. Throughout my childhood, Memphis was a shockingly segregated place, a city full of shorthand codes about who belonged where. The rules were never explicitly stated, but I grew up with an internal map where boundaries were clearly delineated. Barbecue joints, grocery stores, churches, parks, debutante balls—there were black ones, and there were white ones, and that was it.

As a brown girl, I had a hard time knowing how to navigate my hometown. My parents could not advise me; they were themselves relative strangers to Memphis and its racial codes. They had immigrated to the United States in the late sixties from India and settled in Memphis in the early eighties. They moved into a lily-white suburb, on a block where we were the only brown faces, and sent me to an elite private all-girls' school within city limits, rendering my world almost exclusively white, black only around the periphery.

Because of the way Memphis is set up, it was possible in my girlhood (and still is, though harder now) to spend my time interacting only with white people, in predominantly or exclusively white spaces, despite the city being majority black. I was a resident of a white world, but I never felt as if I belonged in it, nor was I sure that I wanted to. I came of age not feeling fully at home in either black or white spaces. I had no comfort zone, no set of known or boundaried territory, no institutions or precedents related to my life, no mentors or public figures who looked like me, no mirror. Instead, I received funny looks that I tried in vain to convince myself were my imagination whenever I left my house and endured such a regular rotation of casually racist assumptions, questions, and insults that I still vaguely dread interacting with strangers in public. Even though Memphis's strange racial dynamics didn't apply directly to me, I got tangled up in them. When you are the anomaly, everyone feels free to comment.

People in my hometown often assumed I was mixed race, since my mom is fair skinned and my father had dark skin and I fall somewhere in between. Depending on the person and how they learned the truth—that my parents were both Indian immigrants and I was their biological child—they would seem either disappointed that I wasn't the product of a mixed-race marriage or pleased that I belonged to a category they considered to be "better" than the one they had previously assumed I belonged to. Both of these reactions were problematic in their own way, though at the time I couldn't have articulated why. Still, I was clear on one thing: no one knew what to do with me.

When I was about seven or eight years old, my mom and I were buying shoes for me at the Stride Rite inside Oak Court Mall, at the time considered a "nice" place to shop (read: mainly white, with some black employees). I was standing in the aisle when a white boy, maybe a year or two younger than me, pointed me out to his mother and used the word "nigger." My own mother was out of earshot, so when she returned and saw me crying, I had to explain why. My immediate feeling was a visceral, white-hot shame—I'd never heard anyone speak that word aloud before, let alone at me. I knew it was a very, very bad thing to say, and I felt ashamed for having triggered the saying of it. It was also clear that this word did not belong or apply to me; I'd been insulted, but not properly. I remember covering my face with my hands while my mom insisted we continue to try on shoes, trying to move past the incident. As I recall, no words were spoken between my mother and the boy's mother—though I seem to remember his mother shushing him in mild embarrassment and alarm—and this made me angry. I resented being made to act as though nothing had happened and was indignant that my mother hadn't confronted the boy's mother and made some kind of impassioned, dramatic speech about equality before whisking me off in the style of all the 1980s-era books and PSAs about *Standing Up to Injustice!* I'd been exposed to.

When you're a kid, your ability to comment or reflect on your own experience is limited. You take things at face value; your experience feels inevitable, not subject to critique, question, or comparison. Still, you learn quickly that your otherness will never be forgotten, even if you manage to forget from time to time what it is that people see when they look at you. Though by many measures I thrived in a white world, I also clearly saw the disconnect between the stated values of American society and its actions in a way only an outsider can. Even if I didn't have the language for what privilege was or what it might mean, I could see that my white classmates moved through the world differently from the way I did. They were raised not to see color, so they didn't think about the fact that when they invited me to their country club birthday party, I would be the only non-white guest and the only non-white person there who wasn't an employee. Even if it did occur to them, they had no way to appreciate what kind of position that would put me in because they'd never been in the minority in any public space, not once in their entire lives.

The white, upper-class Memphis that I knew existed inside its own bubble, its own self-sustaining world with its own set of rules. Preppy was the only acceptable way to dress, and the popular girls all got David Yurman bracelets for their sixteenth birthdays and had boyfriends who wore deck shoes and popped-collar polos. There were a handful of acceptable college football loyalties, and two or three acceptable places to register for wedding gifts, but a wedding reception at the University Club was basically a no-brainer. Memphis money is old and big on tradition: white-dress debutante balls, the Cotton Carnival, the whole nine yards. Concern for or about the "rest of" Memphis arose only when the bubble was threatened, say with the issue of school redistricting or a perception of "unsavory elements" suddenly appearing in neighborhoods previously considered safe.

Most of the rich white people I knew had at least one important black person in their lives: their housekeeper. The love and devotion to these individuals was real but did not extend to a broader demographic concern. And all too often, a relationship that was inherently imbalanced (employer to employee) was considered a shining example of one's own tolerance and open-mindedness.

My alma mater, St. Mary's Episcopal School, now boasts a minority enrollment of twenty-nine percent, but growing up, I was one of a few handfuls of brown or black girls. Over the course of twelve years, all of the classroom teachers I had were white; the adults of color I remember encountering on campus were maintenance or cafeteria staff.

My counterpoint to this white world was the rich soil of chosen family where everyone was brown like me. Before my birth, my parents had built a community of fellow Indian immigrants all transplanted to Memphis, where they began to raise families. My "uncles" and "aunties" (as I called them) and their children were—and still are—who come to mind when I think about my family, even though I'm not related to a single one of them. This chosen family constituted my other life, my evening-and-weekend self, the girl who ate food with her hands and wore *salwar khameezes* to temple and didn't eat meat on Tuesdays as part of her religious observance. I did not show up as that girl at school because it didn't seem wise to do so. Compartmentalizing became my coping mechanism, one that I would again employ as a young adult, when I realized that I was queer. I didn't know the term "code-switching" back then, but I sure was doing a lot of it, moving back and forth between various behaviors: identity as assimilation, identity as flag-waving, identity as shame, identity as shield, identity as weapon.

As a nerdy brown girl with thick glasses and frizzy hair, I didn't have many models for how to be brown inside my particular social context—I had to serve as my own guide. There were no Indian cultural icons to speak of and barely any Asian ones; what did exist landed firmly in the category of stereotype. *Sixteen Candles* ranked high in the rotation of beloved films for high school girls of my generation, but the character Long Duk Dong made me profoundly uncomfortable, as I feared that I would somehow be implicated by his cringeworthy accent and behavior. Other movies that featured prominently at weekend sleepovers—*Steel Magnolias, The Cutting Edge, Girls Just Want to Have Fun, Dangerous Liaisons, The Princess Bride*—featured no characters of color whatsoever. This meant lots of improvisation on my part and a fair amount of guessing—could I dress up as Cher from *Clueless,* or would everyone automatically assume I should go as Dionne, who was black? Did I have to model my outfit after one of the nameless Asian girls who appeared in the background of the film?

I discovered quickly that friends and even many teachers would adopt whatever tone I set in regard to my difference: Was it a big deal? Not that big of a deal? Could we joke about it? I had to offer instructions but do so in a way that wouldn't offend anybody. Many immigrant kids are made explicitly aware of this context and its attendant responsibilities—*what you do reflects on all of us, so you have to represent us well.* To do so requires constantly checking yourself against the standards of two cultures, neither of which you belong to completely. This is a form of the double consciousness that so many people of color naturally adopt, and it is exhausting, even as it becomes second nature. And when you live inside of a social matrix where you are one of the few (if not only) members of your tribe that the mainstream will encounter, it becomes even more necessary for you to show up, in your brown skin, a certain way.

For nearly all of my years at St. Mary's, I took that responsibility seriously—working "twice as hard," as my mom had instructed, to prove that I was "just as good." Because I was eager to learn, conflict averse, and self-motivated, school worked for me; I was good at it. Those same traits made it tricky for me socially, when I took at face value the need to explain or contextualize myself for others, to cheerfully say, "That's okay!" when fellow students, or even faculty members, did things like mistakenly assume my family worshipped idols or that I would have an arranged marriage. I cultivated my identity as Very Helpful Girl, always willing to give others the benefit of the doubt, always happy to share about my culture even as I started to resent being treated as a one-woman diversity show. I learned to anticipate implications that I might have received something—a spot on the mock trial team, an end-of-the-year award, admission to a competitive college—because of the color of my skin. As deeply as I resented the notion that I had not fairly earned the academic success I worked so hard to achieve, I learned quickly that to question these judgments, to object or draw attention to them in any way, would be viewed as unforgivable ingratitude. "Ugh, you're so *lucky*," a classmate said as we discussed our college applications. "They're going to see your name and let you in."

I have long had a complicated relationship with my Indianness. As a young girl, I was proud to be brown, proud to share my culture with anyone who expressed curiosity about it. I liked having something that set me apart, that made me interesting by association. Of course, "interesting" is not the same as "cool," and in middle school I learned how "interesting" could quickly translate to "different" and become a liability. As an only child, I didn't have any trailblazing older sibling to look to for wisdom or a younger one to advise or navigate these complexities with.

Because I was a kid who fiercely loved her parents, I didn't want to feel ashamed of or embarrassed by anything associated with them, but I still did. It felt cowardly and disloyal to wish that my mom would pack sandwiches or Lunchables instead of leftover tomato rice for lunch or to be annoyed when my dad sang Hindi songs while taking long baths on Sunday afternoons instead of playing golf. On some level, I loved those things about my parents; I found them endearing. But I was also always thinking about how their quirks looked to others, how they came across to my white classmates. I stuck out in all the wrong ways, and my brownness was one part of that. My parents were older than almost everyone else's; my mom worked outside of our house (while the vast majority of my classmates' mothers didn't); I was not even a little bit athletic and never played a school sport; I genuinely liked school; I was one of very few only children I knew; I seemed to connect better with teachers than I did with my peers. But while some of those things shifted—whenever my classmates got to know my parents, they found them as endearing as I did—my brownness was immutable and impossible to hide. In second-grade art, we were tasked with making clay angels that were put on display in the cafeteria, and mine was the only one, out of dozens and dozens of angels, that wasn't blond. She had long black hair, just like me.

There were no modes of representation other than the ones I created for myself, pieces I would collage from the broader culture and rework to make them fit. There were no Indians anywhere—not in books, on TV, or in magazines. Not being represented occurred as a complete inevitability, but I didn't seek out representation in traditional Indian culture because it felt even more foreign to me than the white American culture I wanted so desperately to see myself in.

The first mainstream movie that felt even remotely connected to my own life was *Bend It Like Beckham,* which was released when I was twenty-one years old. Though I'm not British, Sikh, or a soccer player, it was still the closest thing I'd ever come to seeing someone on a big screen who vaguely resembled me, and the experience was so moving that I cried. I saw how I missed out on so much of the rich inner lives of my parents and my friends' parents, because I saw them the same way the white broader culture did, discounting them because of their accents and otherness. How shameful that I had never considered my own story to be movie-worthy, to discover as an adult that the uncles I'd thought were goofy and uncool performed complicated brain surgeries and lectured internationally, or to realize that I'd underestimated my gossipy, talkative aunties, only to learn about the multiple degrees they held (because American universities wouldn't accept their "foreign" master's degrees when they'd immigrated) and the three or four or five languages they spoke. It's a raw deal to internalize the stereotypes of the very culture that never embraced you fully.

When I graduated from high school, my yearbook superlative was "All-American Ethnic Girl." And the worst part is, *I'm the one who came up with it.* None of my white classmates felt the need to designate themselves the "All-American Girl" in contrast, or by way of complement, which is what makes it so interesting to me that no one said anything about my choice or encouraged me to drop the "ethnic" and simply go with "All-American." Adding "Ethnic" was a preemptive qualifier, a way to prevent anyone from questioning my worthiness to the title. Claim it before someone can attack you with it or use it against you; that was my strategy.

I was still operating under the assumption that I could construct my own identity and make my own place in the mainstream, that this was something I both *should* want and could somehow achieve. I'd get people to see me for who I really was. I'd be the one to single-handedly hammer nuance into a lexicon of extremes.

My generation was told we could be anything we wanted to be. We came of age singing along to Madonna and Cyndi Lauper, watching *Murphy Brown* and *Designing Women*, witnessing a woman fly into space and being appointed to the Supreme Court. The message of independence was driven home especially hard at my all-girls' school, where we were empowered in ways that made feminism a posture so obvious we hardly ever spoke its name aloud. But this conscious move toward giving girls the tools to succeed and break glass ceilings focused solely on gender. There was no talk about how things might work differently for us non-white girls. Race very rarely entered the conversation when it came to girl power.

As with race and culture, I also straddled two worlds when it came to religion; I like to tell people that I was born into Hinduism but raised in the Episcopal Church. My parents brought me up with a religious identity that included an openness to other faiths. They themselves were the product of tolerant, pluralistic environments, and my mother had attended and taught at Catholic schools in India. They had no fear or hesitation in sending me to St. Mary's, especially because we continued to practice our cultural traditions at home.

It was within the religious context of my childhood that I worked through what it meant to navigate an insider-outsider dynamic. I visited India twice as a child—once when I was so young

that I could not remember the trip—but never felt entirely comfortable being tethered by proxy to the country and its culture at
large. Hinduism, though, I've always felt deeply connected to. The
Hinduism of my childhood was visceral, immersive, and filled
with sensory detail; I loved its emphasis on ritual and practice, the
lush aesthetics of its sacred spaces and depictions of the divine.
When I was growing up, we had a prayer room in our house and
my mother would get up early each morning to read scripture and
sing hymns before breakfast. I often woke to the sound of her
voice, rising and falling in the curve of a familiar melody, sometimes slipping in to join her before getting dressed for school.

Because there was no Hindu temple in Memphis until I was
in middle school, my parents and extended family were my primary source of knowledge about our traditions, explaining rituals and holidays, encouraging my spiritual interest. At school, I
was also encouraged; I was the most enthusiastic student in Bible
class, where I learned about Jesus through Mrs. Williams's felt-
board depictions of his life. I loved chapel, took pleasure in the
quiet time for reflection we were given each morning, but I went
back and forth about whether it was okay to say the "in Jesus's
name" part of the school prayer.

Though I felt drawn to Jesus and his kindliness, I was keenly
aware that he wasn't mine. I didn't want to stop being Hindu, but
sometimes I thought it would be easier if I were a Christian instead, if I could wear a cross and go to youth group on Sunday
afternoons and not have to explain to anyone what I believed. I
felt most acutely out of place on the few days a year communion
was offered during chapel. Though I looked on with a conflicted
sense of longing as my classmates walked up to the altar, I staunchly
refused when friends—even our chaplain—suggested that it might
be okay for me to take communion, too. "But I don't believe," I

said incredulously. "That would be disrespectful." Everyone seemed to like the idea of my being both, but no one could explain to me how I might go about doing it.

Sometimes I coped by exaggerating my "Indianness," placing emphasis on what felt like the most exotic and potentially attention-attracting aspects of my identity. I struggled to figure out what level of visibility made sense. When was I sharing my heritage, and when was I flaunting it? For every teenager, adolescence is a delicate balancing act of demonstrating one's uniqueness while trying also to fit in with the crowd. For me, the "uniqueness" part was easier than for most of the other girls, the "fitting in" much harder. It was with half mortification and half exhilaration that I got dressed in Indian clothes to perform *Bharatanatyam* with three or four of my fellow brown-girl classmates in chapel; I had the same set of feelings when I was forced to reveal to friends that I was skipping lunch because I was fasting for a Hindu holiday. "We have a calculus test today! You should have asked to take it tomorrow instead!"

But I was accustomed to being in the minority, to the world being inconvenient and not revolving around me. Unlike my classmates, who only knew a world that catered to them, I did not feel entitled to any special treatment. I never once had the day off from school for the religious holidays my family observed; our celebrations were invisible to my classmates and neighbors. There were no stores selling Diwali decorations or cards, no mention of it in the news, nobody wishing me "Happy Diwali" at school. We celebrated, but the parties never took place on the actual holy day, because there's no way my parents were going to pull me out of school or take off work.

Learning to make allowances for my family's traditions pushed me to appreciate my heritage more, to understand that I had to

make room for it in my life, to experience firsthand how assimilation can become such an appealing option for immigrants; almost
everything in the dominant white culture is set up to have you
conform, instead of keeping your odd, inconvenient traditions
alive. At times I struggled with the fact that I often identified more
with the traditions that weren't mine, such as our school hymn
sings, where we'd spend an entire chapel period requesting and
singing songs that I found just as beautiful but more personally
resonant than the Sanskrit ones from Hinduism, which I could
sing but not understand.

India always seemed remote and foreign to me. As a child of immigrants, I was careful never to claim the country outright: "My
parents are from India, but *I* was born *here*." My attachment to
India was by proxy, and while I was proud of the paths my parents had taken to bring my hyphenated self into being, India never
felt like mine. The attendant trappings of its culture existed as a
kind of grab bag that encompassed several categories: genuine attachment, inconvenient association, fashionable accessory. My
mom says I used to complain about eating Indian food once a week
as a kid. (I both love to eat and know how to cook that same food
now.) Coming back from winter break in fifth grade with *mehndi*
on my hands was pretty cool, but white classmates asking for bin-
dis after Gwen Stefani started wearing them on the red carpet in
1998 was stressful. None of us knew what "cultural appropriation"
was yet, but I could feel the specter of it pulsing around the edge
of my life.

I struggled with being defined by or limited to my Indianness.
Perhaps my least favorite demonstration of this was when white
people, upon correctly determining or establishing that my family

was Indian, would respond with something along the lines of "We know [insert name of Indian people] in [insert name of faraway state]! Do you know them?" Not kidding. It happened dozens and dozens of times—my parents and I used to joke that one day we were going to respond with "I know these white people in Minnesota! Are they your cousins?"

I was raised to be a good sport—when you're different, you *always* have to be a good sport. Being annoyed or offended is part of your daily experience, and you don't always realize that this isn't necessarily true for everyone else. My parents, immigrants to this country, were clear on the messaging: we would not complain or draw attention to unfair treatment, even if we were sure it was purposeful and somehow motivated by our skin color. They staunchly refused to interfere or swoop in; I had to figure out how to navigate those scenarios on my own, because they knew I'd be doing it my whole life. Though I didn't realize it until later, I was socialized as a brown girl to notice when and how my presence made others uncomfortable—by the time I was ten or twelve, my own discomfort in social situations seemed inevitable.

Likewise, I understood when my presence was being deliberately orchestrated for a certain message or effect. I wasn't ignorant of the visual asset my brown skin provided—I never had to guess why I was routinely selected to be photographed for promotional materials for any school or summer program I attended. But to a second grader, being on the cover of *St. Mary's Magazine* felt like the special attention I craved. Even in high school, I didn't mind being the "diversity card" in my group of friends or realize that I should cringe when a college roommate told me that they'd deliberately revealed to their parents that I liked girls just to freak them out.

The line between appreciation and appropriation is fuzzy, and as a brown person, I often feel like an unwitting Border Patrol agent, never sure which side of the line I'm protecting. Growing up, I found that many of my white friends seemed hungry for pieces of my culture because they did not feel that they had a satisfactory culture of their own. Their identities were convenient but boring. They wanted something to help them stand out or to offer more texture to their identity. I was lucky to have friends, classmates, and teachers who were curious about my religion and culture, and I waffled between eagerly sharing what I knew (at times exaggerating how much I actually knew) and feeling paranoid that my background was the only interesting thing about me.

No doubt it was at least a partial draw for my friends. It became a point of pride when they no longer had to ask for utensils when eating Indian food with my family; my mom gave one of my best friends the nickname "Sangeeta" because of her musical talent and arranged to have a *langa* (ankle-length skirt) sent from India for the graduation gift of another classmate. Only later did I wonder if this was sharing or selling out, granting easy access to the "fun" aspects of my heritage without any of the attendant work.

One of the most beloved traditions at St. Mary's is the annual Christmas pageant, in which seniors who've attended the school since first grade or longer enact a series of scenes from famous paintings of the Nativity, Annunciation, Adoration, and so on. It's old-fashioned and strange and treated with enormous respect by the student body. As a senior, I was selected by classmates to be one of the six Marys—the first but not the last non-white, not-Jewish-or-Christian girl to do so. Everyone called me "Brown Mary," and the church ladies who volunteered for the pageant paired me with another Indian student, Amrita, who served as my Joseph; we threatened to bring in a brown doll to be our baby

Jesus but ultimately dared not. As our humanities teacher pointed out, we were probably the most historically accurate-looking couple up there, though not what Fra Angelico had in mind.

I was sick as a dog in the days leading up to the pageant; the day before, I was running such a bad fever that my mom took me to see a doctor at the critical care clinic. My fever had to break, he insisted, or I could not go into school the next day. (I think I was the first high school patient he'd ever seen weep upon being told *not* to return to school.)

I spent the morning of the pageant in my bed, wrapped up in blankets and shivering, begging my body to be well. Down the hall, my mom performed her daily *puja* (worship ceremony) and I took comfort in the sound of her voice. Singing with her, I felt truly desperate, appealing to the Divine Female on both sides of my personal equation—Durga and Mary—to give me this opportunity to make Christmas pageant history. An hour before the cutoff window for school attendance required to participate in extracurricular events, my fever broke.

The rest of the experience is a rush of feeling and sensation—my beautiful classmates cheering my arrival, embracing me, feeding me soup, doing my hair and makeup, sneaking ginger ale up onto the altar for me to sip as we waited our turns. The collective breath of the younger girls as they paused inside their "Gloooooooooria in excelsis Deo," the heat of the lights inside the tableau box, a sense that the line between reality and something transcendent was blurring, the way Hinduism speaks of: being offered a window into the beyond of our own human experience.

I'd wanted so badly to participate in the pageant because it was a tradition I'd witnessed and looked forward to for years; I did not know that it would also be a rare moment of feeling comfortable inside myself, an opportunity to have the two worlds of my childhood merge, and to be celebrated and embraced, not in spite of any contradiction but alongside of it.

Though I am fifteen years removed from my time at St. Mary's, my compliant, All-American Ethnic Girl self still returns almost as an involuntary reflex. I now teach in a majority-white (though coeducational) school, similar to the one I attended, where I bring many of my previous navigational tricks to bear. I learned long ago that even if you don't know more about India than anyone else, you still become the default expert. Nowadays, I feel much less guilty about saying, "You know what? I have no idea," when asked a question that assumes some kind of intrinsic knowledge of a culture based on the color of my skin.

I find myself looking back and wishing that instead of seeking to make my differences seem smaller, I'd pushed them further in the other direction. I wish I'd known how to make my classmates' cultural biases visible to them, though they were invisible to me as well. I came of age in an environment that emphasized sameness, focused on what we had in common, and refused to speak about—or even acknowledge—anything that was different. Celebrations of diversity involved obliging but distant consumption of other people's cultures and messaging about how we were all "more alike than different." Some would suggest that I should better appreciate the matrix of excruciating politeness and determination not to offend that imbued my formative years, but the net result of that matrix was a sense of liberal, progressive smugness. My white peers got the benefit of feeling enlightened and tolerant without actually having to be so; I was allowed access into their world so long as I didn't force them to give up anything or challenge their perceptions of their own inclusivity.

I was well trained to accommodate the majority, and it is with conscious effort that I now try to interrogate and interrupt those default patterns. One practice I've taken up is the deliberate use of my name, the name my mother chose for me long before I was even born. I don't use a "Starbucks name," something more "typical" or "mainstream" to substitute when ordering a coffee or making a dinner reservation. This is a small act, but for me it has meaning. My name is my signifier, my sign; even the Old English etymology of the word "name" can be traced back to a word that means "to call, nominate, appoint." Names have power—think of how creepy it feels when someone who hasn't earned the right of intimacy calls you by your nickname—and answering to something other than the name I was given, the name that claims me, feels like a compromise.

I'm aware that I might not feel so righteously entrenched in my "no Starbucks name" positionality if my name were more multisyllabic, consonant laden, or at the further reaches of American English pronunciation abilities. Not only does it feel like erasure to forgo one's true name, the same feeling can be achieved when hearing it said incorrectly, over and over and over again. But apologizing for or hiding your name can also be part of a broader posture of trying to take up less space to make things easier on those who've never had to stretch beyond the boundaries of their knowledge and experience. We don't heat up our leftovers at work, because they "smell funny" to our colleagues. It feels conspicuous to talk to our compatriots in our native languages in public, so we don't. I wonder what would happen if we stopped worrying so much about whether we're making those in the majority uncomfortable? It's not from nowhere that white people developed the idea that they are entitled to be comfortable all of the time; they demand or expect it, sure, but we are often the ones who comply.

Black Is the Color of My True Love's Hair

PART ONE: FAMILY AS RORSCHACH TEST

Browsing through babyGap, checking out at Whole Foods, waiting in the security line at the airport, I would always hear the question "Is he yours?"

"Is that your baby?"

"Are you his mother?"

"Are you his nanny?"

Ever since my son started to speak and call me Mama in public, the questions shifted:

"Does he look like Daddy?"

"Is your husband tall?"

Sometimes I'd be bombarded by statements, as if, by the force of sheer declaration, these strangers make sense of what they're seeing:

"You don't look anything like your mama!"

"But Mama isn't very tall!"

"You must look like your daddy."

I am curious to see how Shiv will field these questions when he is old enough to understand and answer them; I know that how he responds will depend in large part on how he sees me respond. Which is why, though I'm tempted, I've resisted the urge to print passive-aggressive "fuck off" note cards that I could hand out at will:

Thanks for your interest in our family!

As it turns out, you've asked a question about something that's none of your goddamn business. You should know better. Don't you know better?

The next time you're tempted to ask deeply personal questions of complete strangers, please try to remember that the world and its possibilities are far bigger than your little narrow purview attests. Check your assumptions. We don't owe you an explanation. Neither does anybody else.

Have a great day!

Friends often try to assure me that people mean well, urging me to go easy on them, to be gracious, to give people the benefit of the doubt. "People don't mean to be offensive," they tell me. "They just don't know how to say it without coming across that way."

What these friends don't understand is that when the act of explaining your family structure becomes a part of every day of your life, you grow tired of being gracious. It's exhausting to have strangers view your life as an opportunity for an educational experience. The underlying message to Shiv is, *You and your family don't make sense to me. You need to explain it to me. You owe me an explanation.*

To be treated like a puzzle is to be reminded that you don't belong. When you are forced to account for your life during even the most mundane interactions, you can't help being reminded of how the rest of the world sees you. In contrast, when the world you occupy is built to accommodate you, you fit inside the boxes. You make sense. You are expected. Your existence is accounted for in paperwork, in pop culture, in legislature. I, on the other hand, grew up checking "Other" on the State of Tennessee forms for years, because the only categories under "Race/Ethnicity" were "Black," "White," "Hispanic," and "Other." I have had to remind more than one nurse practitioner that women who sleep with other women can be sexually active without having to account for birth control. I have written in my own relationship category because "Single," "Married," and "Divorced" didn't apply to me.

When I was younger, I struggled with the entitlement of strangers who brazenly asked about my ethnic background, as though my coloring and features were deliberately designed to infuriate them.

"Where are you from?"

"You have the most beautiful skin!"

"Where are you from— I mean, where were you born?"

The problem is that when asked where I'm from, I will truthfully respond, "Memphis," the city where I was born and raised. But this, of course, is not the answer people seek or expect from me, not what they really want to know.

"Uh, but where is your family from?"

"You're from Memphis?"

"No, where are you really from?"

As if someone who looks like me couldn't possibly be from Memphis. As if, even though I was conceived in and born on American soil, I won't ever fully be "from" here. Now my child still has to field the same entitled questioning that I did. But yeah, we totally live in a post-racial society.

Growing up brown in the South, I learned that politeness was the priority. Sure, my family would acknowledge, you have the right to be angry; your hostility is justified. But to act on it risks ruining things for all of us. Your immigrant parents teach you to be patient, to gently laugh off offensive comments and calmly explain that your family is from India, but you were born in the States. Everything around you—news stories, sitcoms, comments made in line at BBQ shops—teaches that while others project their assumptions, this is not something you can reciprocate because you must remain polite and well mannered. All it takes is one mistake, and it will be counted against you forever.

You are told not to add more fuel to the fire, which ends up adding more fuel to your fire, until one day you find that you are in your thirties and you have a black son and you're a lot less willing to give people the benefit of the doubt.

Our family, as perceived by folks at the grocery store and dentist's office and so forth:

JILL: white, Louisiana born and raised
NISHTA: brown, Tennessee born and raised
Yes, we are a couple. No, by "partner," we do not mean the business kind.
SHIV: black, native Texan, placed with us by his birth mother at birth

Yes, he is our son. No, he did not come out of either one of our vaginas.

Shiv calls me "Mama," while in his eyes, Jill is "Gigi." Jill picked the name before he was born; I was much more attached to the idea of having a "traditional" mom title than she was, and we wanted to avoid having overly similar parent names, as it seemed potentially confusing for everyone. So she picked "Gigi" because it sounds like Jill. My mom, who lives nearby and speaks to Shiv exclusively in Hindi, is "Nani," the Hindi word for maternal grandmother.

Sometimes I marvel at the convergences my son embodies. The other night, he was tucking his dinosaur toys into the basket he keeps them in, and he started to sing the Hindi lullaby that my mom sings to him and sang to me as a child. Here he is, this black kid with two moms, one white and one brown, who turns the heads of Indian families we encounter at the zoo when he calls out *"Hathi!"* instead of "Elephant!"

Our family doesn't fit well into boxes. We don't fit at all. Often, I sense this really sweet and completely awkward desire that some folks have to express that they see and support our family. This is not to say that they "approve," per se, but demonstrates something along the lines of *I think your family is great and I want to convey that, but I'm not really sure how.*

Which I understand. I've felt that way, too. I've told strangers in the park, "You have a beautiful family" without having any earthly idea how that particular group of individuals was linked together, but it being clear to me that they were, in fact, a family, in the truest sense of that word.

Most of us don't have the right language for these situations. Maybe the right language doesn't exist, no way around the weirdness of saying *How awesome that you adopted a black baby!* and, *We are not assholes and we think your same-sex relationship is lovely.* Maybe it seems ridiculous that such statements should even be necessary or notable, except that we know they are and so that's why we say them.

Once, a black male cashier at Whole Foods asked skeptically, "You're his mom?" and I was reminded that what people see when they look at us really has more to do with them than us, a Rorschach test of sorts. When Jill is out with Shiv, it's fairly obvious to most people that she is a white woman with an adopted son. We've noticed that people tend to be particularly affirmative of that pairing, in a way that expresses *How great of you for doing that!* More than once, Jill has been thanked—by black women exclusively—for adopting Shiv. I wear a ring and am dark skinned enough that Shiv could presumably be my biological child if my husband were black; I've never been thanked.

As is well documented, children of color are considered "difficult to place" by the adoption industry, and "difficult to place" children come with a slightly lower price tag. Do I want to use this kind of language to discuss how my beloved son came into my life? Of course not. But, beautiful as it can be, adoption is an industry, with not a small amount of money at stake. My son cost less to adopt because he is black.

Non-white children, particularly African American children, are harder to place in adoptive homes, according to a 2013 NPR article. The majority of adoptive parents, particularly for private adoption, are white, but only twenty-one percent of private adoptions are transracial (the exception being international adoption, where the vast majority of children are adopted from Asia by white American parents). Though not commonly known, many adoption agencies offer different "fee schedules" based on the race of the adoptive child; sometimes, the financial incentive can nudge adoptive parents to consider adopting a child of color.

When Jill, Shiv, and I are all out together, the opportunity for presumption increases exponentially. People do not naturally assume that my family is a family and that Jill and I are his moms. "Who is she?" a fellow parent, also of Indian descent, in Shiv's music class asked me when Jill accompanied us for the first time. "She's his mom," I said. I received a puzzled look before adding, "He has two moms."

I will freely, though not at all proudly, admit that I have been cagey, defensive even, when we interact as a family with black strangers. We had been told by our adoption agency that it was unlikely we would be picked by a black birth mother; their anecdotal experience reinforced the stereotypical ideas I had about widespread homophobia in the black community. I worried that black strangers would disapprove of us being Shiv's parents, that they might carry personal views about who should raise whom that would implicate me.

Despite this, nearly all our reactions have been positive, though at times they've been charged. Over time, I grew more aware that I was, in part if not altogether, creating that charge with my defensiveness; I am guilty of being relieved whenever it doesn't seem to be a problem that our child has two moms, neither of whom look like him. And I know that I am guilty of thinking of Shiv like a badge, like a human "pass" that gets me into some kind of club, even though it doesn't, of course. I would find it undignified to say *I have a black son* because it seems to imply that his blackness is essential to me, but when someone asks about Shiv and I move to pull out my phone and show a picture, is it because I want a special prize for being the mother of a black son?

All social interaction is, on some level or to some extent, performative. We are always performing, always reading social cues and dancing in between them, deciding what we can and can't say, anticipating how others will respond, putting up walls when we anticipate an attack. Judging, perceiving, performing—at least that's what the adults and big kids are doing, anyway. My kid, for now, he's just being: he sits in the grocery cart and is himself no matter where we go, no matter who's around, while all of this troubling and problematic stuff swirls about him.

My mom is very conscious about wanting everyone to know that she is Shiv's grandmother. Her skin is much lighter than mine, which has raised issues ever since she was pushing me around in a grocery cart. When someone stops to say hi or speaks to Shiv in the way that people always do, addressing the baby instead of the grown-up with the baby—because it's safer? because my kid is a giant flirt who likes to smile at strangers?—my mom will drop a comment like "Oh yes, he loves going shopping with his granny."

Part of me sees this as a helpful gesture she's worked out, a way of letting people know how to think about what they're seeing and to respond accordingly. But another, itchier part of me feels *Why do people need to know the nature of their relationship? Why does my mom feel compelled to tell them? What does it matter if strangers assume she is someone other than who she is?*

One of many examples that I remember distinctly: Mom, Shiv, and I out for Mexican food with our friends Greg and Sharon. It was Christmastime, and we were seated by a dazzling, shiny tree, which competed with a giant bowl of guacamole for Shiv's attention. He sat in Sharon's lap, across the table from me and Mom, and flirted with the (white) folks he could see on the other side of the tree. "He is adorable," they told Greg and Sharon, clearly assuming Shiv was their son. I did not correct them— indeed, given the way we have intentionally designed Shiv's "village," he is, to a certain extent, theirs—but I could feel my mom's visceral desire to say something.

I vacillate back and forth: On the one hand, it is hurtful to be othered, especially after a lifetime of othering. I don't want to stand out from the other moms; I don't want to think about my family being different in any essential ways. But I also don't want to be ugly, to assume the worst of people, to create a rift where it doesn't necessarily have to be. Shiv's pediatrician's office is warm and welcoming, and we are far from the only same-sex family there, but their forms still say "Mother" and "Father" instead of "Parent" and "Parent." Every time I'm there, I think, *Should I say something? How much does it matter?* Because it isn't just my little family that this affects, or even just the other LGBTQ families; our forms haven't caught up with what many of our families look like now: with stepparents and single parents and grandparents and foster parents and the dozens of other possible configurations we fail to make room for.

The older I get, the angrier I'm willing to allow myself to be. We limit and harm people when we affirm these categories over and over and over again.

PART TWO: WELL-MEANING WHITE PEOPLE

They truly are color-blind. My former primary care physician is the kind of doctor lots of people dream about having: personal and warm, but also professional, kind, and genuinely connected to her patients, with a well-run practice full of people who are wonderful to interact with. Laura is smart. Laura is thoughtful. Laura is educated and well read.

So I was flummoxed in our recent conversation during which she related to me a story from a mother-daughter book club meeting she had attended. The moms and girls had read a book set in the antebellum South, where race was obviously a topic of the discussion. All the book club members in attendance that day (including my doctor) were white, save for one young girl who is Latinx and was adopted by white parents.

"The kids didn't even think about the fact that Maria isn't white! It was amazing," Laura said. Indeed, it is *amazing*. It is amazing that anyone could convince themselves that it is even possible—let alone preferable—to raise a child to the age of ten without any consciousness of their own or anyone else's color. It is amazing that these adults saw it as positive that it did not occur to their children that this conversation about race might feel different for their friend of color. I wanted so badly to ask what it had felt like to Maria.

There are certainly by-products of color blindness in modern society and friendship that are fairly harmless; in college, my very pale friend Elizabeth once asked to borrow my concealer before a dance, unthinkingly. "You can borrow it, Liz, but I don't think it's going to be very good at concealing anything." But this, of course, was a betrayal of her privilege—she didn't think about it because she doesn't have to think about it. She doesn't have to choose carefully which drugstores or Target she walks into, for fear that makeup matching her skin or products for her hair won't be available.

These are the things that I think should be obvious by now—the ones that I feel like enough people know that I forget not everyone knows them. There are still hordes of well-meaning white people who like to trot out the line "Oh, I don't see color!" or the less well-meaning ones who argue that I am making "too big of a deal" out of this conversation about my family and race.

"Not seeing" color is, of course, a form of privilege; it means that things are oriented around you and others like you. It means that you can walk into almost any bookstore in any neighborhood in America and see pictures of people who look like you on the cover of magazines, find books for your child with families who look like yours. Indeed, it means that you would never know not to expect this or to mark it as noteworthy. The ability to "not see" color comes only when the society you live in is not constantly shoving your color down your throat, reminding you of your otherness through benign or not so benign ways. For the rest of us, even if we wanted to, not seeing is never an option.

PART THREE: ALL OF THE THINGS WE DIDN'T THINK ABOUT

I'm sitting across from Jill in a coffee shop that used to be a gay bar. "The last time I was in this space, there was very different music playing," Jill muses over her mug of single-origin, responsibly sourced beans. Just across the street from where we sit is a four-star restaurant that used to be a lesbian bar—another sign of gentrification. With mainstream visibility comes a loss of separate, safe spaces. For some, this is positive, a sign of acceptance and arrival. But I wonder what we lose by getting lumped in with everyone else—always this question of assimilation. To be fair, Jill and I like—and frequent—the restaurant a lot more than we did the bar, which was kind of a dump. We are old and past our bar days anyway. Today we're here to debrief from our first tour of a preschool we're considering for our son.

We're looking for a place where our child can learn and grow and be safe: eat snacks, play, get dirty, make friends. Because of our background as educators, we're looking for a school, not a day care, and furthermore for a school where our family will be a welcome addition and not an anomaly. Add to this our financial constraints and the fact that we're looking for a partial-day, two- or three-day-a-week option, and the choices grow even narrower.

Then there's the diversity concern, which is what we're discussing in this coffee shop. There are lots of things we love about the school we just toured: location is great, accreditation is top-notch, and the teachers and programs are very high quality. But there aren't any black kids. Okay, there are maybe six. Out of several hundred students, there are six black children. Is this a deal breaker? We don't know. We know it moves the school down in our rankings as we weigh the options. "I mean, the only way they're going to get more black kids is if parents of black children send their kids there, right?"

I grew up in the minority—one of a few children of color in a majority-white school—but even that seems different, since the demographics and serious lack of integration in my hometown would seem to lend itself to such a scenario. But Houston? The fourth-largest city in the country? Then the question arises, would this matter to us if our child were white? We feel like it would, but it's so hard to say now—not only is it hypothetical, but we are also raising a black son, an experience that has forever changed the way we see the world.

It's hard trying to figure out how not to be an essentialist and also how to be mindful, aware, in reality: to see the world for how it really is. And so sometimes we struggle, as we are in this conversation about where to send Shiv for preschool. "I don't want to make his color into some determining fact about him," I say. And it's tricky to imply that race or the absence of racial diversity necessarily means any one thing in particular, though it tends to coexist with certain things I don't want. Visibility matters. I want my son to see others who look like him and see them as his equals, not only as maintenance or security staff. Am I trying to create a false world for my child, a world that doesn't exist? Does that make me just as guilty as the white families who are doing the same?

My father died unexpectedly when I was twenty-three, and for a long time I divided the world into two kinds of people: those who had dealt with grief and those who had not. If you lost someone very close to you—best friend, parent, sibling—and at a relatively early age, there are certain things I knew you would "get," that I wouldn't have to explain to you. Jill and I have learned that the same holds true with this: there are two kinds of people, people who have black sons and people who don't. For Jill, this distinction has been especially world altering. Her sense of her own white privilege used to be furious and intellectual but now is blood-boilingly visceral. It has been a shock and a revelation and has drawn her closer to the black people in her life as she seeks them out for guidance, asking questions and trying to understand. For their part, these friends have generously welcomed Jill as a newly baptized ally, sometimes with even a literal arm around the shoulder and a "Welcome to our world."

The truth is, there are people out there who get it, even though they don't have black sons. There are people who feel our terror at the specific threats the world holds for black men and boys, even though they know they don't experience it. The people who understand that "praying for healing" is not good enough, who realize that white guilt is really just indulgent privilege and doesn't do shit to change anything anyway. The people who think to send notes of solidarity, who understood why I showed up at work during much of August 2016 with eyes glazed over and dazed from staring at #MikeBrown and #Ferguson tweets all night because I couldn't bear to look away, because it was only my privilege that allowed me to be a spectator that night.

For Shiv's first Christmas, we took him to see Santa twice: the first Santa was white, the second was black. We were prompted to make the second visit by a black friend of ours, who gently informed us where we might find a Santa who looked like our son at a local art gallery that features work by African American artists. I debated briefly whether we should make a point of taking Shiv to see a Santa of color. On the one hand, of course we should, but on the other hand, it felt so antithetical to the way I'd been raised as the child of immigrants: to conform to the white experience.

But that was precisely the point. When we became Shiv's parents, we promised that we would push ourselves to be thoughtful about our choices, to remain open to learning and growth, even—or especially—when that learning challenged our preconceptions or pushed us to do things that made us uncomfortable but were clearly best for Shiv. In the end, I figured a second visit to Santa would be a fun way to spend a Saturday morning, and we'd get some cute pictures out of the bargain. Which we did, which we then posted on Facebook.

"I loved his picture with black Santa!" our white friends said, immediately confirming to me that going had been the right choice. The color of the Santa whose lap your child sits in might not seem to matter, but when the dominant image of male blackness in this country is of the dangerous, violent "thug," a gentle, smiling Santa is like a revelation. Because when our friends said "black Santa" instead of just "Santa," they meant that Santa, like Jesus and all powerful good men, is by default white.

One of the realities I've had to confront as Shiv's parent is the fact that, for many people, he represents an innocent incarnation of male blackness that people take great pains to affirm and admire: the good, safe, right kind. There is often a transactional twinge to it all, as if loving on my sweet little black son now somehow assuages the guilt of future judgment of him when he is big and tall and strong and eighteen and they will cross the street to avoid him, or post on Nextdoor when he lingers in front of their yard, or clutch their purses a little tighter when he enters an elevator.

When he was first born, mothers of the students I teach would stop me in the halls and demand to see pictures, peering at my phone with their faces already broken open into wide-mouthed smiles. They had heard from their children that my baby is cute, but their kids have been so well trained that they never mentioned my son is black. The moms would see his face on the screen and their mouths would stay open just a fraction too long, because they didn't want to betray their surprise or say something stupid. "Oh, he's so cute!" they would say, meaning it, but then it would quickly start to cross the line into overpraise, as if they were going out of their way to comment on his handsomeness to assuage themselves of their shock. "Where'd you get him from?" they would ask, as if inquiring after a pair of shoes.

PART FOUR: MORE STORIES WE TELL OURSELVES IN ORDER TO LIVE

When I was growing up, my mom used to tell me that to parent meant to constantly worry. "You just wait," she'd say. "Someday, when you're a mom, you'll understand." Except that my mom had very little to worry about as far as my physical well-being was concerned; I was never actually in any real danger. I grew up in a ridiculously safe suburb made possible by a degree of economic privilege that, statistically, made me one of the safest children on the planet. My son is growing up inside a similar kind of privilege, but it will not have a similar impact on his statistical safety. Because he is a black male living in America, the threat of violence looms no matter what we do.

All parents have to face the reality that we are not ultimately in control of what happens to our children. Despite the statistical improbability of misfortune, my mother's worry about me wasn't completely unfounded. Accidents happen. People get sick. The world can be a scary place. But it feels very different to know that because of the color of my son's skin, the world is a different kind of scary for him. A parent's job is ostensibly to protect, but can I really protect Shiv when I also need to prepare him for the reality he will soon face?

I spend most of my thirty-second birthday inside the bubble of my middle-class, professional privilege. I go to work, where my (mostly white) students are extra-sweet to me and assure me I'm "not that" old even though I'm twice as old as them. I hear from friends and family throughout the day on Facebook, via email, in text messages. I teach class, grade papers, plan my family's Thanksgiving menu, go to meetings, and head home to spend time with my two-and-a-half-year-old before Jill and I head out for a nice birthday dinner. We drop our son off at his grandmother's and head out to enjoy wine and four-cheese pizza topped with locally sourced prosciutto, talking in that luxurious way that comes when you find yourself across the table from your spouse of a dozen years, without your toddler in tow.

When we get home, I check Twitter and find that the grand jury in Ferguson has made the decision not to send Darren Wilson to trial. Once again, I watch my feed bloom and ripen with photos and Vines of protesters and police on West Florissant, broken glass, tear gas, and the desperate anger I feel with them: my heart a bruised, deep purple anguish. In that moment, I am glad that our son is sleeping elsewhere, because I know I would risk waking him just to slip into his room and see him, tangled in his big-boy bed, one hand clutching his beloved puppy, breathing even and rhythmic. I know that I would want to touch him, to feel his realness, to imagine how I could ever stand upright again if someone were to take him from me. I tell myself that I will be able to find a way to keep him safe, that I am giving him things that will protect him. I tell myself these things even though I know they are lies.

Working the Trap

*Queer is a continuing moment, movement, motive—recurrent,
eddying, troublant. . . . Keenly, it is relational and strange.*
—EVE KOSOFSKY SEDGWICK

Reading before bedtime is a sacred ritual in our house; our son has two educators for parents, so books have been a part of his life since day one. When he was still tiny we could make it through one or two board books in the rocking chair before he started to get sleepy. As he grew, he became more and more engaged, picking out the books he wanted, going through phases of favorites, pointing to and identifying objects and animals in the illustrations as he learned the words for them. These days, he is big enough to sleep on the bottom bunk of a "big-kid bed," and that bottom bunk is big enough to hold our entire family—two moms, one child, and two dogs—during bedtime stories. An old, battery-operated lantern that used to be reserved for hurricane season provides the light that we read by, and Shiv is allowed to pick three books every night. (He often begs for more, so we sometimes relent and read four.)

One of the books in his regular rotation is *And Tango Makes Three,* which tells the true story of two male penguins at the Central Park Zoo who spend all of their time together, show each other affection, and sleep next to each other every night. When these penguins (Roy and Silo) see the other (opposite sex) penguin couples caring for an egg in their nests, they use a rock as a stand-in for an egg and take turns tending their own "nest," even though it produces no baby. After the human penguin keeper observes this, he decides to bring the couple an egg in need of raising. And so the first same-sex, adoptive penguin family is born.

As in most children's books, the allegory here is anything but subtle—*gay people love each other the way straight people do and they want to be parents just as badly, and when they are given an "egg" to raise, they do so carefully and lovingly.* (It was this very didactic rhetoric that moved many to ban the book from library shelves and schools.) The narrative is compelling; I cried the first time I read the book aloud to Shiv, both the ache of wanting to be a parent and the joy of finally becoming one translating perfectly across species. But the book's intent to normalize families like mine—conveyed via the phrase "just like," which is repeated half a dozen times throughout the book ("just like the other couples," "just like the other families")—makes me a little bit itchy.

Gay families! They're just like us! reminds me of the *Stars! They're just like us!* features in gossip magazines, with photos of celebrities doing "normal" human activities such as walking dogs, exercising, getting ice cream with their kids, strolling down the street wearing sunglasses, and the like. *Isn't it amazing?* the copy notes. What's amazing is the idea that you could ever compare the experience of someone whose candid photograph is routinely sold to and printed in magazines with mine. These magazine features serve only to further highlight the degree to which celebrities' lives are decidedly *not* like ours.

In similar fashion, the overarching rhetoric around LGBTQ acceptance has insisted on sameness, both stated and implied. But this insistence rounds off the sharp edges of differences that should not be ignored. There is clearly still a divide if you can walk into any bookstore in the country and find dozens of books about families with a mother and father, but in order to read books that deal with families who look like mine, you have to track down the handful of titles and special order them; if you have to routinely edit paperwork, crossing out "Father's Name" on medical forms and school forms; if your friends have to edit store-bought cards, moving the apostrophe to say Happy Mothers' Day for the plural possessive; if you didn't get to take your boyfriend or girlfriend to prom; if coming out still carries real risks to your relationship to your family, your safety, your employment; if your same-sex family is still not guaranteed all the same legal rights as straight families; if you once again find yourself correcting a stranger (the receptionist, or the insurance broker) who assumes that because you checked the "Married" box, you have a husband— you are reminded, over and over again, that you are not like everybody else.

Is my family "just like" straight families that we know? In some ways, yes. We love, play, worry, frustrate each other, create weird little rituals, snuggle in the bed on weekends. But I don't want my worthiness to be judged on the basis of whether I live up to someone else's default standard, whether I "do family" in ways that straight people can recognize or approve of. As Rumaan Alam, author and member of a two-dad, tricolor family, wrote in a 2016 *New York Times* op-ed, "Respect should not be reserved for those who adhere to some notion of convention." I want to be respected even when I don't play by everyone else's rules.

The "just like everyone else" trope was a key hinge in the pro-marriage equality argument; heck, it *was* the pro-marriage equality argument in its essence. *Hath not a Queer eyes? If you prick us, do we not bleed?* This kind of rhetoric has a long history of softening hostile majority groups enough to allow minority groups to make important gains; it becomes a kind of "shame into tolerance" strategy. The problem, of course, with a moral argument predicated on sameness is that it does not necessarily force anyone to work through the fear of difference at the root of their intolerance. I see a similar limitation in the "born this way" insistence on homosexuality not being a choice. If our acceptance is contingent upon our being unable to help how we are, what we earn is pity for being the way we are, not necessarily the right to be that way, whether we chose it or not.

I have noticed that straight allies tend to trot out the "they can't help it" argument more than most queer people I know, who understand sexuality as being a little bit more complicated. But allies of all stripes eat up sound bites, stand stubbornly by black-and-white declarations that allow them to come across as morally righteous. And straight people love being allies, or thinking of themselves as allies, changing their Facebook profile picture to glow with that special rainbow overlay. After *Obergefell v. Hodges,* which legalized gay marriage nationwide, they showed up at Pride in droves to bask in a victory that wasn't about them, ally babies in tow. Straight people love going to Pride in much the same way I think they love going to New Orleans: because it's fun as shit, is a little bit transgressive, and comes with a tourist's day pass into a culture they find fascinating and "exotic."

I sound bitter, I know. It's not that I don't appreciate the support of so many real people in my life who truly care about the legal rights and well-being of my family. But I do resent being expected to appreciate shows of support that are mostly, well, for show: for the coolness points and the "right side of history" points and the "pat yourself on the back" points, without any real knowledge of the issues at stake. There is little risk, at this point, for straight white liberals to identify as LGBTQ allies, which is I guess why I'm not necessarily impressed when they do it.

Queerness isn't something you can put on or take off, not a magic kingdom you can visit for a day and then leave, taking your rainbow souvenir back home like some kind of trophy rewarding you for your open mind. The problem with the "just like us"/shared humanity argument is that it fails to go far enough past polite acceptance into the radical kind. And I worry that our emphasis on sameness has lessened our ability to tolerate difference. It has become startlingly clear in this country that respectability is no guarantee; just because you can get married or drink out of the same water fountain as everybody else doesn't mean that deep-seated cultural disgust has been erased. And disgust is rooted in the very fact of our difference, the fact that we live inside of a society that was not built with us in mind and does not know what to do with us, except to tell us to be "just like" them.

When my wife's cousin came out to his mother decades ago, she told him, "Be gay like Jill." Jill has a good job. Jill has a long-term partner. Jill lives in the suburbs and pays her taxes and buys her jeans at Gap and doesn't shove her gayness in anyone's face. She doesn't wear it on her sleeve. The way she expresses her sexuality allows you to forget that she's different.

Of course, even if *you* sometimes forget that we're not straight, we don't. We can't. We are constantly being reminded that to say too much or do too much may cost us our jobs or our business or even our safety. I can think of two or three times (in fifteen years) that Jill and I have held hands in public. I once had a colleague tell me that I was "taking it too far" by mentioning my partner in candidate interviews we were doing as part of a search committee. "You could really turn someone off of coming to the school, doing that." Several of my (straight) colleagues had also spoken about their spouses in the same interview sessions. I work for a school with "sexual orientation" in its nondiscrimination policy (a deliberate choice), but parents still complained that it was "too much" for sixth-grade students to hear me mention my female partner's name or see her photograph on my desk. After two years, I was moved up to teach eighth grade, where ostensibly it was less potentially scarring for students who already knew I was gay to be reminded of my gayness.

That's always the message: You can be gay as long as you aren't *too* gay. Or you can be gay in private. We'll let you stay if you live a compartmentalized life; keep the freaky stuff where we can't see it. I used to be abashed by flamboyance when I first came out, not sure that I wanted to claim everything that came with the community I would now be identified with. Growing up brown gave me a lot of facility in trafficking in the model minority mythology: how you can gain what feels like real acceptance by presenting yourself as the exception to just enough of the rules, letting those around you think of themselves as accepting without the burden of having to be inconvenienced. In high school, while I spoke to the administration privately about what it felt like to be queer inside those hallways, I did not push for a change in the rules so that I could bring my girlfriend to prom, as my straight classmates urged me to. I went to Memphis Area Gay Youth meetings, which were private and confidential, but did not march with them in the Pride Parade, which in that city at that time was still much more transgressive than cool. Queer pride, according to scholar and poet Maggie Nelson, is "a refusal to be shamed by witnessing the other as being ashamed of you." I wasn't there yet.

It was, to be quite honest and at the risk of sounding daft, love that pushed me to realize that my reservations were a product of revulsion, of internalized homophobia and expectations around gender performance. I fell deeply in love with Jill but still struggled with bringing her home to preppy-as-hell Memphis because she was not the superfeminine lesbian who would have fit more easily into the space of my hometown's expectations. So shamed by being ashamed of her, I faked at not giving a fuck for long enough that the defiance started to feel like my own. Then, for years afterward, I deliberately chose not to vocalize my "from afar" attraction to butch women, trans men, and genderqueer bois because I worried about getting pigeonholed both ways—straight people who would perpetuate a stereotypical understanding of same-sex relationships as being "imitative" of opposite-sex ones, gay people who would erase the complexity of my attraction in order to place me in a particular category. This changed when I came to love and care for friends who were transitioning or reconstructing their gender identity and were hungry for the very affirmation I was holding back. I am forever grateful to the queer community in Tucson, Arizona, who welcomed me as a young graduate student, cared for me as I grieved for my father, and taught me that my freedom is dependent upon the degree to which I can confront my own discomfort about the broader society's perception of me.

So much is riding on our ability as a society to give up the notion that we are entitled to be comfortable all the time. For the minority, of course, comfort is not an option. You learn to identify the cues of strangers responding to your visible difference—refusal to make eye contact, edging away should they be forced to stand near you in line, tight-lipped grimaces when you smile at their baby. Over time, I've toggled back and forth between various survival mechanisms, assimilation versus anarchy, not dissimilar to the process of working through my feelings about ethnic identity, which I've been reckoning with for longer. Being first-generation Indian American has also meant moving between the two poles of assimilation and rejection of the dominant culture, but being brown is not something I can hide, nor is it something I have to declare. It simply is. Being queer has proved slightly more complicated.

When I first came out, I was determined to hold on to my "good Memphis girl badge," to prove that I could kiss girls and shave my head but still be considered acceptable. I hadn't yet heard of the model minority, but I sure was trying to be one. I took pride in being able to pass, slipping back seamlessly into the straight world I'd been raised in, properly dressed and well spoken, the girl who would make grandmothers say, "She's a *what*?" and maybe change their minds about the categories I occupied. But I soon learned the limitations of this approach—instead of changing the rules of belonging, they just make you the exception that proves the rule.

Looking back, I know it was my dad's death, coupled with the community that surrounded me in Tucson, that offered me some freedom when it came to exploring a more authentic expression of my sexuality and self, pushing past the norms I'd been raised with and developing something else. He, more so than my mother, objected to my being gay, and grieving for him meant wrestling with this issue that went unresolved with him when he died. At the same time, because grief is so all-consuming and exhausting, it often blocks out space for other things, things you maybe weren't all that committed to all along, like caring what other people think. Grief and the public expression of it already make people uncomfortable—we are not good, culturally, at sadness—so I had less to risk by letting go of my self-censorship and attempts to play nice.

My friend Marynelle has a long history of being a "fag hag," a straight woman who keeps the almost exclusive company of gay men. (Like many in-group terms, its connotation is affectionate to one set of people and deeply offensive to another.) At her wedding, my date—my friend Phil, who is married to a woman—and I were seated at the table of forty- and fifty-something "choir gays" who have gone to the same Memphis church as Marynelle's family for decades; they are doctors and lawyers and organists and have mastered the art of navigating a society that prefers to pretend they don't exist, except as needed, for show. They have carefully cultivated acceptable personas—smart, funny, gracious.

"Why are gay people always more interesting?" Phil asked, not sarcastically, as we drove away at the end of the night. "I *never* have that depth and breadth of conversation with straight guys."

Why are we more interesting? Because we have to be.

A few months after getting married myself, I saw Alison Bechdel, award-winning cartoonist and acclaimed graphic memoirist, give a keynote presentation at a teachers' conference, wryly noting that we queers "made ourselves obsolete" via our attempts to be treated "just like everyone else." Indeed, Bechdel's own *Dykes to Watch Out For* cartoon strip grew out of her desire to see women like her reflected somewhere out in the world, but after twenty-five years of Bechdel celebrating and attempting to normalize it, that otherness had disappeared enough to make the reason behind the cartoon no longer seem relevant. So she stopped drawing it: victory or defeat?

We have made it to the mainstream. I mean, Alison freaking

Bechdel was a keynote speaker at the National Council of Teachers of English Annual Convention, which meant that the word "dyke" was floating around that auditorium in a way that felt downright radical by virtue of its lack of scandal. But something is lost in the transfer.

Maggie Nelson says it best:

> *Once something is no longer illicit, punishable, pathologized, or used as a lawful basis for raw discrimination or acts of violence, that phenomenon will no longer be able to represent or deliver on subversion, the subcultural, the underground, the fringe, in the same way.*

The day of the *Obergefell* decision was, without question, one of the happiest days of my life. I'd had a reading the night before, which had gone extremely well and given me the chance to spend time with several of my close friends, at a bar, after dark, on a weeknight—a true rarity in my life as a parent of a young child. One of those friends, Megan, an attorney and SCOTUS nerd and the person responsible for introducing me to Jill, is the one who broke the news of the decision to me in a text message that next morning as I drove Shiv to school. As a rule, I try not to look at my phone while I drive, so I didn't even notice until I reached down to play "Baby Love," at Shiv's request, on his Spotify playlist. I saw Megan's text and immediately started crying. Jill was in an all-day session for work, but I texted her anyway. She wrote back with more exclamation marks than she usually uses in an entire month and asked me to marry her.

I wanted to get married—I wanted what "everybody else" had, or at the very least wanted it to be made available to me. Jill and I both wanted Shiv to have parents who were married, wanted the legal protections that marriage would afford us. We had done without them while Jill was diagnosed and treated for cancer and when we adopted Shiv, and we keenly felt the weight of uncertainty and the tang of bitterness that comes when you do not have paperwork backing you up.

Three days after the *Obergefell* decision was issued, Jill and I nervously walked into the county courthouse in downtown Houston. We weren't sure what to expect: Lines? Protesters? Resistance? Refusal? Instead, we got a clerk named Maria, who, after filling in our personal information and making us raise our right hands to swear it was all true, nonchalantly mentioned that her daughter had gotten married a few years prior, when same-sex marriage had been made legal in a nearby state. She smiled at us, took our money, stamped our license, and sent us on our way. The whole thing took maybe twenty minutes.

Having steeled ourselves for the worst, we giggled incredulously on our way out of the building, halfway expecting someone to come running after us and insist that there had been a mistake. "That's it?" we marveled. "Man, no wonder straight people keep screwing this up. It's *way* too easy to get married."

The relief of not having to fight, not being excluded, not having to push or challenge or ask to see a supervisor—it was sweeter than we thought, that relief. Even when you've long made peace, or some semblance thereof, with the inevitability of living well outside the mainstream, you can't help feeling good at being welcomed back in.

As a blue-eyed, blond-haired, obedient little girl, Jill was regularly conscripted to be the flower girl for weddings, often for people she didn't even know. She was soon turned off to the whole idea of weddings; it all felt false, artificial. Plus, there is absolutely nothing about the "Princess for a Day" fantasy that appeals to her. Though she couldn't quite put her finger on why, when she was young she never imagined herself standing in front of a church in a white dress, getting married to a man. That wife of mine, not a fan of weddings.

The irony is that I *love* weddings. I love attending them, crying during them, dancing after them, helping other people plan them. I am kind of a fool for ritual and enjoy stereotypically pretty "girl" things. I love Indian weddings best of all, because they are in their own Technicolor stratosphere of the celebration universe. Indian weddings are bright and vibrant and joyful and last for days and are such tremendous spectacles that there's no pretending they're not completely ridiculous, in the best way. But I never wanted one of my own. Not even when I thought I was straight.

For years, I'd been told how "mature" I was, how unlike other people my age—an occurrence I both resented and cherished. Because of this, I believed that I would be single for a very long time. (I routinely told my parents to be prepared for me to become a single parent if I made it to thirty unmarried.) I believed that *if* I ended up finding someone, he would probably be some smart older man, the Professor Bhaer to my Jo March. I always imagined that he would be white, seeing as how I was not anything close to the "ideal" Indian girl that Indian guys seemed to be attracted to. White people were everywhere, and a white guy had been deemed acceptable, though not of course preferable, by my parents. (It's also important to acknowledge that I was the product of an American culture that did nothing to bolster the potential appeal of Indian—or any Asian—men. I did manage to have crushes on a few Indian boys . . . they just never seemed to be interested in *me*.)

I didn't bargain on the fact that I would end up in a relationship that landed even further outside the expected parameters than "older white guy." With Jill in the picture, a wedding seemed so far off the table that I put it out of my mind as a possibility. I didn't even talk to my parents about my relationship with Jill for years; if only my younger self had known that I would have happily taken the family fights over how many people to invite and what to put on the dinner menu, if it meant my parents celebrating my relationship. When my straight friends complained about their mothers or mothers-in-law driving them nuts with wedding planning, it was all I could do not to gripe at them that at least they *could* get married. And while I admit to being jealous of more than one Williams-Sonoma registry, what I really wanted was not a wedding itself, but everything that it stood for and represented—the celebration of the relationship, the acknowledgment of the commitment, the solemnity and sanctity. When you say you're getting married, people show up. They make plans; they buy plane tickets. They bring you presents. They make a big deal.

The word "wife" has always creeped me out—it just felt so contractual, so old-fashioned, so . . . straight. I never, ever wanted to have anything to do with it, and it would grate on my nerves when straight people used it in reference to themselves or other straight people: *Let me check with my wife* or *So excited to become his wifey!*

I could never really explain why it bothered me so much (the word "wifey" and hashtag #wifemeup bother me still, but that I *can* articulate), but the clue was contained in the fact that before we were actually married, I found it kind of sweet when straight people would use the word "wife" to refer to either me or Jill. A colleague: "I was hoping to meet your wife at the holiday party." The host at a dinner party: "Oh, is this your wife?"

It was thoughtful, and I got what they were trying to do, the respect they were trying to connote, but it still felt like play-pretend. Jill and I were adamant about not using the word "wife" because, according to the U.S. government, that word didn't apply to us. Until it did. Now I love referring to Jill as my wife. It's so *convenient*. For thirteen years, I stumbled over what language to use when talking about her, or introducing her, or just casually discussing my life. "Partner" seems logical, except that it confuses lots of people who think you mean "business partner" (especially straight people who read you as straight and live in Texas and/or Tennessee and don't have any LGBTQ people in their life, or at least think they don't). I refused to say "domestic partner," which sounds so clinical, like a condition you can treat with a prescription drug. "Girlfriend" was too trivializing—it took Facebook a while to figure out that I did not want to characterize my relationship using the same language my eighteen-year-old students gave to theirs—and "beloved," which someone once suggested to me, felt way too intimate for daily use. "Spouse" seemed like the best possible option but still felt like compromise. When you say "wife," everyone knows what you're talking about, even if they're going to raise eyebrows about it. And, you know, it *is* nice to be part of the club. It is nice when my friend Christian texts and says the Old 97's are coming to town and his wife is on board for the show and what about me and my wife? It is cute when my students grumble that the head of school referred to Jill as my "partner," because we're married now and he should have said "wife."

We even used the word "wife" in our marriage ceremony: *I joyfully take you as my wife*. What has happened here? Are we complete and total sellouts? Was my hatred of the word "wife" motivated by jealousy all along? We have newly married straight friends who feel the inverse; they hesitate to use the terms "husband" and "wife" because they carry too much weight, too much history of what those relationships look like. But we don't have a history of gay marriage to avoid or imitate. We're making it up as we go.

I grin every time I look at the band I wear on my left hand or look over and see the same ring on Jill's hand. Is this what it feels like to drink the heteronormative Kool-Aid? I learned not to want something because I thought I could never have it, and now I do—my version of it, anyway. But there are still so many things that we, as a community, do not yet have: employment protection, transgender rights, safe schools. Even before it happened, I knew my marriage was no Band-Aid, but I worried that it would be seen by many as one. I worry that our long focus on marriage equality means, now that we've obtained it, we'll be told to "be grateful" for what we have and fall in line. I don't want to be placated. I want access to the mainstream, but I also want the right to live outside of it if I choose.

Queering has always been about challenging, troubling, questioning. Perhaps it seems hypocritical to challenge, trouble, and question the territory that you are also demanding access to, but without the continual movement that queering brings, we risk ossification, the stiff bones of stasis. All any of us can do, argues philosopher Judith Butler, is "work the trap that one is inevitably in."

Voluntarily Bald

My father asked me to grow out my hair about a year and a half before he died. He didn't know he was about to die—this was not a deathbed request—but it wound up having the power and intensity of one. When you lose someone, their words take on weight, become sticky, viscous, more difficult to disregard.

He asked me to grow out my hair because we were going to India, traveling there as a family—him, my mom, and me—for the first time in twenty years, and he wanted my hair to be "not so short" when we arrived. He had always preferred my hair long and never tried to hide this preference. He was good-natured about it, like he was about almost everything, and our banter about my hair became a running family joke:

"Nito, why don't you grow your hair long?"

"Daaaaad, if you want long hair, grow it yourself!"

My dad went bald at an early age, so this made for a reliable laugh. There was a sharper edge underneath it, though; he really *did* want me to have long hair, and I really *was* annoyed by his persistence. Disagreements between parents and kids regarding appearance, whether it's hair or clothing or piercings or tattoos, are universal and often not about the adornments themselves but rather about what they signify. Inside my father's frame of reference, for an Indian girl to have long, flowing hair was a sign not only of beauty but of compliance and social acceptability. Short hair was "American," a sign of my assimilation and, by extension, his failure to raise a more "traditional" daughter.

When he was alive, I never thought consciously about the fact that a beautiful daughter can serve as a kind of cultural capital for fathers, but I did chafe against the notion that my value was necessarily tied to my appearance and also, by some not-explicitly-stated-but-not-difficult-to-extrapolate correlation, my marriageability. Even inside our liberal group of immigrant families, marriage was always an expectation, a necessary component of how success and the good life were defined. Within the families of our immigrant community, my generation was almost all female. We grew up with the understanding that while our parents were happy for us to find our own partners—the American way—and they might even be able to make room in their imaginations for a partner who was white, the idea that we *would* get married, preferably around the age of twenty-five, and subsequently produce grandchildren, was decidedly not optional. This was such a default expectation that I'm not sure any of us ever thought through what would happen if we didn't get married or didn't want to.

In what might seem like a contradictory stance, our parents also expected us to take up professional careers, pushing and challenging us as students and supporting us in graduate school, just as they saved to pay for our future weddings. (Savings bonds purchased upon the birth of a baby girl are not uncommon in the Indian community.) And though the preference for sons within Indian culture is well-known, my father never displayed that preference. Even at the height of our estrangement, I never felt that he wished he'd had a son instead of a daughter. He grew up with two older sisters and held a deep reverence for them and his mother, who died when he was in high school. Having witnessed firsthand the gender-related obstacles that Indian society put in front of the women in his family, he had consciously chosen a strong woman (my mother) to be his wife and defied others' expectations when he "let" her work as a teacher even after they were married.

With me, he was a "you can do anything you set your mind to" dad, bragging about my grades and engaging me in political discussions and debate from an early age. He was, by any measure, a man who loved being a dad and an active parent. He told me he loved me all the time; his affection came easily. I felt safe inside of our relationship, appreciated and praised for my intellectual capabilities, challenged and supported in my academic and extracurricular pursuits. But my appearance was always the sticking point; in addition to hair, my weight was a concern. He never outright shamed or degraded me but dropped a lot of thinly veiled comments about whether I'd exercised on a given day or whether I "needed" to have dessert. I know that health and genetics were at least partial reasons for these remarks—my father had type 2 diabetes and underwent triple bypass surgery when I was a freshman in high school—but nevertheless I hated them. I did not see myself as beautiful, and this occurred like a personal failure; nothing from the outside world seemed to reflect a sense of that beauty back. In the very white company I kept, I felt freakishly other, and not in an interesting, exotic kind of way. In my Indian immigrant extended family, I was known as the smart one—smart, but not particularly pretty. I was proud of being smart, but I also wanted to be seen as beautiful, wanted others to see me in a way I could not see myself. Instinctively, though, I knew that I should not betray this desire, knew that it was shameful to want this. Though beauty clearly came with its advantages, the language of *it's what's on the inside that counts* was all around me. I never stopped longing for the kind of attention I thought being beautiful would attract, but, pragmatically, I knew that smart was my wheelhouse, the realm inside which I was most likely to receive praise, so I focused on that.

Around the time I got my driver's license, I chopped off all my hair. Having worn it shoulder length or longer throughout middle and early high school, and having had various levels of success with my frizzy curls, I found a pixie cut daring and freeing. It was an aspirational haircut, a style that belonged to the kind of person I wanted to be: bold, sassy, fun. I undertook this change in style around the same time that I developed my first really close friends, people who "got" me, around whom I felt comfortable being myself. In them, I found a group of people who gave me permission to be weird (it didn't take much in my relatively homogeneous high school environment), and my haircut was a way of signifying and celebrating that difference. To wear my hair short was to reject a certain kind of adolescent femininity and, consciously or not, also a way to give the middle finger to my father's beauty standards, standards that weren't just his but also reinforced by every American magazine and Bollywood movie I ever saw.

My father wasn't just the main man in my life; he was essentially the only man. In addition to an extended family network full of daughters, I attended an all-girls' school from grades one through twelve; only one of my close friends had a brother. I didn't spend much time around boys until my friends started dating them in high school, and I didn't make a close male friend of my own until college. I felt wary around boys. It seemed like I needed to be someone other than myself in order to relate to men, or in order for them to be interested in me.

I went through several unrequited crushes on boys who were all older than me (a trend that would continue into adulthood) before I became conscious of my attraction to women. I came of age in an environment where female affection, including displays of it, fell under the umbrella of "normal," so I may well have had earlier crushes that went unidentified. There's also a chance that I resisted the pull of female attraction because, once I gave in to it, I felt like a cliché: the girl who hadn't had any luck with boys who then wound up liking girls. I didn't believe in cheap causality, but I worried that other people would.

In the moment I realized I was falling for the girl my best friend was dating (yes, I know, it was not ideal), I was stunned. I was the straight one in my group of friends; we even joked about it. Being queer—I wouldn't have used that term back then, though it would have been handy, since calling yourself "bisexual" meant no one took you seriously—was not a possibility I'd considered for myself.

I never stopped liking boys, but dating a girl, as I did my senior year of high school, freed me from the awkwardness I had previously felt with men. I no longer felt the need to attract their interest or earn their approval; I wasn't so worried what they thought of me, whether they saw me as pretty or wanted to kiss me. I didn't need them anymore, so I was finally able to enjoy hanging out with them.

Coming out may have improved my relationships with guys, but it was fairly detrimental to my relationship with the one man who mattered most: my father. When I came out, it seemed to validate the fear behind his complaints about my hair and also his belief that my sexuality was a choice, one that I was making deliberately to inflict harm upon my parents—first-generation rebellion gone extreme. *Was* my short hair really the first step in coming out? *Should* we blame my twelve years at an all-girls' school? I was choosing a different life from what he had envisioned for me, one that seemed a direct rejection of the values and beliefs he and my mom had assumed I would adopt as a matter of course.

I never had a sit-down-on-the-couch, planned-and-deliberate coming-out conversation with my parents. Instead, I kept my relationship with my high school girlfriend a secret for the first few months. I was afraid, not only of what my parents would say but also that telling them would spoil the newness and joy of my first time falling in love. Instead, I relished coming out to classmates, teachers, and friends, nearly all of whom responded with the joy and affirmation I craved. But since I've never been able to hide things from my mother for very long, eventually she realized that I was keeping something from her.

What was hardest for her, strangely, was the fact that she hadn't seen it coming. She has long prided herself on her "sixth sense," especially as it related to me, so she felt thrown for a loop that something was taking place that she'd never even imagined as a possibility. She'd thought my strange behavior and behind-closed-doors phone calls were about drugs. When I told her I was "just" kissing a girl, I asked, surely that was preferable to smoking pot? Apparently not.

For as long as I could remember, my mother was my confidante, my coach, and my toughest critic. Her own mother died when she was a toddler, and she despised the stepmother who'd taken my grandmother's place; as a result, she made it a point to develop closeness and trust with me, sometimes at the expense of closeness and trust in her own marriage. While she was not thrilled about my dating a girl, she was willing to wait it out, to hold off on issuing a definitive response, convinced that this was "an American thing" and hopefully just a phase. For this reason, she urged me, conspiratorially, to refrain from coming out to my father. We would keep it between us—no sense in creating drama if it wasn't going to be an issue in the long-term.

Looking back, I know I should have rejected this power play, should have hashed things out with my father sooner. Of course, what I didn't know was that he would live for only five years past my high school graduation; my time with him was limited. Not knowing this made it easier to move away from him, to convince myself that the distance was a normal part of growing up, to feel thrilled by the secret keeping and sense of independence it brought me. I spent a lot of my senior year apart from my parents, driving from school to friends' houses or to my girlfriend's apartment, feeling freer and more capable than I ever had, popular and interesting and under the impression that this was essentially what adulthood felt like.

Though she was the one who had insisted we not tell him, my mom wound up outing me to my dad in February of my senior year. She and I were in the middle of some kind of fight—about what, I have no memory—and my father came to my defense, which was not uncommon. My mom and I clashed regularly in my teenage years: I exerting, she pulling back, my dad mediating. In this instance, his defense of me sent my mom over the edge, and she countered by revealing the piece of information she'd been hiding, a piece of information clearly intended to discredit me and upset him: I was dating a girl.

After confirming this information with me and processing his initial shock, my dad's first tactic was to sit me down in the living room for a serious talk, his default first tactic. Serious talks, when they happened in our house, took place in the living room. The only other things we used that room for were piano practice (me), Saturday morning newspaper reading (my dad), and taking pictures of family dressed up for some kind of occasion.

I think my father thought he could talk me out of being gay—at least, he tried. He seemed to believe that if he simply explained to me the hardship and difficulty I was causing my parents, the ungratefulness that my "choice" demonstrated, then I would stop dating my girlfriend, or at least agree not to date any more girls after this one. When I refused, he stopped speaking to me for three months.

I met his anger, withdrawal, and indignation with my own. There are few creatures more righteous than I was as an eighteen-year-old; my father's desire to raise a strong, independent woman with convictions came with unintended consequences. I didn't even bother to try to persuade him. I'm not sure if I thought he would come around eventually or if I was simply protesting on principle. The bond that had long existed between us broke.

Things were tense in my house for the first time in my life. During the last few months of my senior year, as I received college acceptances and won awards at graduation and made plans to accept a merit scholarship offer to attend Rice University in the fall, I grew more accustomed to seeking affirmation and community outside of the world my parents had built for me. I still loved my nuclear family, as well as the extended Indian community I'd grown up in, but I had begun to see its limits. I started to conceptualize myself outside of and apart from my native environment.

Overall, my coming-out experience was fairly mild; I wasn't kicked out of my house, I wasn't cut off financially, I didn't face any violence, nearly all my friends and teachers were supportive (at least in theory). The break with my father, though, was painful. His coldness felt like the worst kind of betrayal. Maybe his love was unconditional, but it didn't seem like it. To make matters worse, I dated a guy during my first semester of college. He was the first guy I'd ever had a crush on who liked me back, which perhaps had something to do with the moxie I'd gained as a woman with some relationship experience. We dated for a few months, my one and only heterosexual romantic relationship. Short-lived as the relationship was, it lasted long enough for my parents to get their hopes up; they met him over Parents' Weekend and were smitten.

I, on the other hand, was not. By Thanksgiving, it was clear to me that my boyfriend was more emotionally invested in the relationship than I was. He was talking about someday-babies while I was still stuck on my ex-girlfriend. After winter break I broke it off, and a few days later I shaved my head. I know, it seems like another terrible cliché. But the act was not wrapped up in any man-eschewing, radical lesbian sentiment; my partner in crime in this adventure was my best friend and roommate, Rebecca, who is straight. The head shaving was her idea.

In college, Rebecca was much less of a conformist than I was— even before shaving her head, she was often misread as a lesbian, thanks to all of the stereotypical boxes she checked: lack of makeup, almost exclusive preference for pants, familiarity with tools, cars, motorcycles, and construction. She'd already shaved her head once before, and it was her boldness that inspired me to shave my head along with her, to see if I had the guts to go through with it. I did.

The whole thing was like a double-dog dare to myself: *Let's see if you can be as ballsy as you want to be. Let's see if you can let go of what other people think long enough to see what could be possible when you do.* What I didn't anticipate, and what was perhaps even more emboldening and useful, was what it meant to deal with everyone else's reactions to my hair (or lack thereof). Some people—almost always men—would come right out and ask, searching for a narrative that made sense to them. Were Rebecca and I cancer patients in recovery? Had we shaved our heads in solidarity with a cancer patient? Were we joining the military? The idea that we'd shaved our heads simply because we wanted to, because we wanted to see what would happen if we did, boggled a lot of minds. My parents were likewise flummoxed, though they took it more in stride than I'd anticipated. They thought I was nuts, but they weren't angry; head shaving confirmed the theory, perhaps, that I was in a phase of experimentation that was not destined to last.

For me, a shaved head served as a kind of litmus test. At a time in my life when I was examining old friendships, sorting through which ones would last and which ones might not, people's responses to my hair were helpful data. Likewise, as I worked to create new relationships at Rice, I was able to determine quickly who cared about what. But there is perhaps nothing more significant about shaving my head at nineteen than the fact that I met Jill not long after I did it. When I showed up as a student in the Intro to Comparative Religions survey course that she team taught, she thought I might be a Buddhist nun; I thought she might be the single most charismatic person I had ever met. I fell in love with her quickly, though it took me a while to realize that's what it was. Jill and I both had the matrix of "teacher crush" in mind until it became clear that our connection was in a category by itself. By the end of my freshman year of college, I knew that Jill—nineteen years older than me and, whoops, also my professor, and, double whoops, already in a relationship—would be my forever person, even though I had no idea what that would look like. I also had no idea how to tell my parents.

It was pretty clear that I wasn't going to be marrying any men, so it seemed necessary to disabuse my parents of the notion that I might, lest they become too hopeful that my sexuality was "just a phase" after all. Leaving out any mention of Jill, I came out to my parents a second time, in what was surely the world's most ill-advised phone call, the *I'm gay for REAL* conversation. Needless to say, it did not go well.

Throughout the rest of my time at Rice, my relationship with Jill solidified as her previous relationship ended, but it still remained a secret from my parents. They did not know that I alternated between backyard dinners at her suburban home (now *our* suburban home) and late-night library sessions and parties on campus. Jill and I began to introduce both sets of our friends to the idea of us as a couple, and we were met with some skepticism but also a fair amount of support. When I traveled with her to Shreveport to meet her parents, I was introduced as a "friend." When my own parents came to visit Houston, I introduced Jill as the same. Once, she and I traveled to Memphis without my parents knowing we were there, staying at a Hampton Inn five miles from the house I grew up in. Sitting in that hotel room, drinking Jack Daniel's Country Cocktails with my friends Wayne and Caroline, who were meeting Jill for the first time, I felt a lot farther away than five miles from my parents.

By the time I graduated from college, I'd had enough separation—literal and emotional—from my parents to commit to rebuilding my relationship with them. So when my father requested that I grow out my hair in advance of a trip to India, I was more open to considering the request, which I might have previously dismissed out of hand. He must have known that, too; our relationship had been strained for nearly five years. On some level, I was a twenty-two-year-old who missed her dad, missed the magic of being Daddy's little girl, missed living in the era before I had disappointed him so thoroughly.

That was the allure of his request—if I agreed, I would be doing something for *him*—perhaps paving a path back into his good graces. Fully committed to Jill, I knew my relationship wasn't going to change; my hair, though, was up for grabs. I'd become more confident in my identity, and my hair didn't necessarily need to serve as any kind of statement. So I stopped cutting it, and by the time our trip to India rolled around, I had managed to get it to chin length.

There was something powerful about spending three weeks in India and being surrounded by both media advertising and real-life images of women who looked like me. They were beautiful in a way that did not seem so completely separate from me; they were the kind of women that my father, with his long-hair obsession, had wanted me to resemble all along. I understood for the first time what he saw, or wanted to see—I understood the appeal. In a strange twist of perspective, I found myself drawn to the idea of being that archetype, the curvy Indian girl with long, enviable hair. She felt achievable. She felt like me.

Less than two months after we returned from India, my father died, from a by then untreatable pulmonary fibrosis, which was discovered on the Fourth of July. He was hospitalized, seemingly out of nowhere, and once admitted, he never left. He died on July 22, 2006. In a turn of dramatic irony, after my father's death, my hair started to fall out. This is a common enough response to acute stress, but it didn't seem coincidental to me. In most cultures, hair is shorn as a sign of mourning, but that was the opposite of what my father would have wanted. So I grew it long instead, past my shoulders and down my back, relishing the knowledge that I was doing something my dad would have liked. There is so much uncertainty in grief, so many questions about the proper response to something so awful; keeping my hair long was one way to concretely mark myself as fundamentally altered by my father's death. Plus the work of it—caring for it, spending time and money and energy on it—gave me, in my sadness, something to do.

The dead can have even more power over us than the living. When my father was alive, defying his preference by keeping my hair short was part of our dynamic, problematic though it sometimes was. But grief renders relationships one-sided and fogged by memory. Growing my hair long was a way of staying tethered to my father. After six-plus years of keeping it that way, I no longer knew whether it mattered, whether it honored him or was keeping me from letting go.

I wound up saying goodbye to long hair a few months after my son was born—with a tiny, nursing newborn and a full-time job, I was interested in making my life less complicated. Donating ten inches of hair, I reverted to the low-maintenance (and babyproof) pixieish cut of my late teens and early twenties. The pragmatism of the decision helped assuage the guilt I had over my father's hypothetical reaction. Was *I* the betrayer now? Ultimately, I managed to convince myself that my father would have been so pleased at having a grandchild that he would not have been the least bit bothered by my hair: such is the imaginative calculus of self-justification.

I shaved my head for the second time the summer Shiv turned

three. He cheered me on as I guided the clippers over my head. "Mama, you ain't got no hair! We match!" At the time we were keeping his short, too, due to a proclivity to roll around in the sandbox at school.

When you are a woman in your early thirties who shaves her head for no apparent reason—well, people want there to be a reason. As was the case when I had shaved my head a decade before, no matter the reason behind it, a shaved head invites speculation about who you are, whom you love, what your "agenda" might be. This is not without consequences. Having a shaved head moves you outside the conventional definition of what an "attractive woman" looks like, which means I get flirted with a lot less. I am a big flirt, so this is a bummer; men just don't look at me the same way without hair. In fact, most of the men in my life initially responded to my shaved head with humor, the kind that's usually masking discomfort or a sense of not knowing what else to say. They don't seem to understand why a woman would want to cut off her hair voluntarily, without some really compelling reason, as if *wanting to* weren't reason enough. It reminds me of how straight people sometimes react when they learn that, technically, I consider myself bisexual; I am attracted to women, yes, but I am also attracted to men. I don't actually consider myself "born-this-way" gay, but that narrative seems much more palatable to much of society. After all, if I had a choice, why wouldn't I have chosen *their* kind of life? If I could have had a man, why did I choose a woman?

On the flip side, I've never gotten so many compliments from women in my life. Not in a flirtatious way, though; the vast majority of the women I hear from are ones I read as straight (my gaydar is pretty good). *Oh, I love your hair,* they'll gush: in the bathroom at the gym, in the aisle at the grocery store, in line to check out at a hotel. They call my hairstyle "brave," express envy at how easy it must be to take care of. *It looks so good on you,* they'll say. *I wish I could get away with having hair that short.*

I try to tell them that they can and that they should; I spend so much less time thinking about and dealing with my hair. It. Is. Glorious. But it's also a reminder of the strict boundaries women have about how they look and whether they fit into a general standard of what's considered attractive by white, heterosexual society. My hairstyle is an attempt to feel free from, or at least partially removed from, these stereotypes, like a matrix from which I can unhook myself. Of course, the jig is that, even as a queer woman, there is no unhooking, not really. I remember looking at myself in the mirror about a year ago and thinking, *You look like a big ole dyke,* which is, for all intents and purposes, kind of what I am. But it throws me a little, the knowledge that I present that way. I feel like the same person inside; in fact, I'm more confident and happy in myself than I've ever been. And yet I still want that external validation.

Which is why I haven't grown my hair back out yet. For one thing, it sounds like way too much trouble—I'd need a lot of convincing to add more time onto my morning routine and more money into my personal grooming budget. Pragmatics aside, I want to test myself a little longer. My students tell me my shaved head makes me look intimidating, like I don't give a shit, and I tell them that was the whole idea. I have never thought of myself as being particularly badass, but my haircut makes me look like I am, and in moments, I feel like it, too. I'm living into my hair, or the version of me that goes with it.

Wrestling with Ghosts

Being the first-generation daughter of Indian immigrants means that I have learned to avoid Urban Outfitters, the clothing and tchotchke bazaar for twenty-somethings, because there's inevitably going to be an image of something I find sacred being hawked to college students without so much as a caption to acknowledge the appropriation: Shiva on a pillow, Ganesh on a wall hanging. It means I have learned that most yoga studios are, ironically, hostile places for brown people, because of the butchery and false interpretations of a practice that, for me, is rooted in Hinduism and not about looking good in lululemon pants. I have likewise learned that anything associated with India, especially food, is going to be described, inevitably, as "exotic" and probably also sexualized, as if spices could somehow be "sultry." I have long since given up on explaining that the complicated religious concept of karma can't actually be reduced to "what goes around comes around." I have watched the food media act as if they're the first people in the world to discover cardamom, when I've been putting it in my tea since childhood. I have felt intense guilt when white people have seemingly more claim to my culture than I do, with their knowledge of Sanskrit and Ayurvedic medicine. I have discovered that being first-gen feels like living on a seesaw, constantly going back and forth.

Most other first-gen kids I meet feel the same way—I use the term "kids" even when referring to adults here, because a key aspect of the first-gen experience is constantly defining yourself in relation to your parents. Arguably that's true for everyone, but I think when your parents are mirrors of the dominant culture, it's easy to misjudge or altogether miss just how pervasive their parental influence is, even on decisions and choices that have seemingly nothing to do with them. For first-generation kids, though, it's pretty obvious what was passed down from our parents, what we rejected from our parents, and what we simply absorbed from the dominant culture.

There is a certain amount of recognition among first-gen kids, even if our families are from wildly different places; our experiences, values, histories, and stories tend to have several strands in common. If you're first-gen, you know what it's like to be a kid trying to navigate a culture without any help from your parents, because they grew up somewhere else. You've experienced the stumbling, vacillating back-and-forth urges between conformity and rebellion, in response both to the dominant culture and to your parents' culture. You've felt annoyed by strangers who ask, "What are you?" or by romantic partners who exoticize and fetishize you or teachers who want you to serve as a representative for an entire culture, country, or religion to the rest of the class.

Until my mid-twenties, a bindi was something I wore only on "Indian" occasions—that is, any occasion that called for wearing Indian clothes. When I was a kid, this consisted of religious holidays or trips to the temple, gatherings of our extended family, weddings, that kind of thing; very rarely did I wear my Indian clothes out into the white world. The clothes and their accompanying bindi were like a costume of sorts, one that I put on when it was time to occupy the Indian part of myself. In a sense, a bindi is an apt metaphor for my relationship to my Indianness, something I kept putting on and taking off, something that made me feel simultaneously embarrassed and also proud.

Growing up, I was always so glad that my mom was not one of those sari-clad Indian moms at parent-teacher conferences or in the grocery store. I had friends with moms like that, and I felt bad for them. My mom was a liberated Western woman with two master's degrees and a job outside the house. She wore pants, but she also woke up early each morning to perform *puja* in the prayer room in our home, down the hall from my room. I would often wake to hear her chanting in Sanskrit, occasionally joining her to kneel in front of images of Ganesh, Shiva, Durga, and others, accompanying her as she sang the *aarti* (hymn/prayer). She fasted on Hindu holidays, waking up extra early to prepare special foods and iron the Indian clothes we would wear later in the day, after we'd been to school and work. Having lived in America since she was twenty-one, she navigated all kinds of cultural details seamlessly, in a way that I found dazzling. Her depth and breadth of knowledge, especially as it related to food, was something I always aspired to have myself. Not only does she make homemade yogurt, using a culture she smuggled from India, but she also makes killer shrimp creole, *dosas,* and spaghetti sauce. She taught me how to make a mirepoix around the same time she showed me the proper way to start a *vagar*. In the kitchen, my mother modeled how I might occupy multiple cultural spaces at once.

Though I'm not sure I did it consciously, I followed her lead when it came to balancing the different parts of my identity—neither sentimental about nor ashamed of my Indianness, but also careful not to let it be the dominant feature by which I was known. After all, my mother was the one who decided when I was born not to speak Hindi to me, afraid that I would then grow up speaking English with an accent and face the same judgment and discrimination she and my father had. Though she, like almost everyone who grows up in India, is multilingual—English, Hindi, Punjabi, Urdu—she opted to raise a monolingual child.

I have deep shame about not speaking Hindi. This is primarily an adult feeling; as a kid, I was content to understand the basics: colors, animals, foods, how to write my name. In a sense, I understood my experience as inevitable; in the group of Indian families who formed our extended family, there were several other kids who didn't speak their parents' languages either. The ones who did had learned by necessity via grandparents who came to stay for extended periods of time, grandparents who didn't speak any English. But I didn't have any grandparents in my life—both of my father's parents had died by the time I turned five, and my mother is essentially estranged from her father and stepmother. By the time I wished that my parents had chosen differently with regard to my language, I was already a teenager, way past the window for sounding like a native speaker. What's more, my parents were so accustomed to speaking in English, even to each other, that asking them to switch to Hindi didn't really work. There was no chance of taking Hindi at my high school, though I did try in college, but to be honest, I didn't push very hard to locate resources that might help remedy my linguistic lack.

The older I got, the more that "not speaking Hindi" became conflated in my mind with "not being Indian enough." I'm not sure if the origins of this linguistic gatekeeping were wholly imaginary or based on a true sense of disappointment on the part of others, but I do know that my failure to fully master the language mirrors my ambivalence about my identity. Difficult things do not generally intimidate me; when motivated, I research and fall into obsessive rabbit holes and self-teach and commit myself to building new skills and habits. But my sense of the impossibility when it comes to learning Hindi is based on fears far beyond any actual effort that might be involved.

The last time I tried to learn the language, I was a graduate student in my early twenties, anticipating a long-planned trip to India with my parents. It would turn out to be the last trip we would ever take as a family of three—not something we knew at the time, but still a fact that adds to the drama and significance of the story. Six months before we left, I asked my parents for a set of Rosetta Stone DVDs for my birthday and practiced with them rather faithfully until we left. While in India, I didn't speak much Hindi—I've always been very self-conscious about my accent—but I did understand quite a bit of what was being said. Filled with a sense of accomplishment, I returned home determined to continue my progress. I pulled out my old books from college, asked my mom to correct my pronunciation and explain grammar rules I didn't understand. I downloaded Hindi language learning podcasts. And then my dad died.

Everything about my sense of identity shifted after my father died; not only did I have to work to figure out who I was without him but I also had to do so while already in the midst of defining myself in that really messy way that is characteristic of most people's early twenties. I wanted my father's death to change me irreparably, or rather, I knew it would, and I wanted to let it, wanted to lean into and intensify that change. Somehow, I decided that it would be impossible, pointless, to learn Hindi without my dad.

My grief about him became conflated with grief over a language I would never learn.

In nonlinguistic arenas, embracing my Indianness was the primary way I connected to and sought to honor my dad after his death. Because my father was a person who loved to eat, I decided to become a person who loved to cook. Food was, and still is, a way for me to throw out an existential tether across space and time. Plus, cooking is practical; it gave me something to do and a way to connect with people, both things you really need help with when you're in the throes of grief. In the months following my father's death, I spent hours on the phone with my mom, asking her questions as I tried to re-create dishes in my tiny grad school apartment kitchen. I subscribed to food magazines, threw my first grown-up dinner party, and set out to master any dish I knew my father had loved or that I thought my father would have liked.

To suddenly be whipping up batches of *rajma* (Indian-style red beans served with rice) and be in possession of a spice *dhaba* (steel spice container, ubiquitous in Indian kitchens) just like the one I'd grown up watching my mother use felt both wonderful and strange; I had distanced myself from many of the markers of my Indianness while in college. Coming out as a senior in high school had thrown me into a bit of a predicament regarding identity. In the first eighteen years of my life, I had worked to create my own sense of what it meant to be first-generation and brown, adopting, adapting, and rejecting the various models around me. There weren't many, but there were some. Then, when I realized that I wasn't straight, I saw models for what *that* life might look like, both in the broader culture and in my friend group, but my models were all white. The trouble was, I didn't see any way to reconcile the two. Being brown *and* queer made me feel like a true anomaly; I'd never even heard of other brown people who weren't straight. (Though I knew that it couldn't be true, at times I felt like I was the only queer brown girl on the planet. My parents seemed to think so, too.) I felt myself presented with no other option than to leave my Indian identity behind for a time while I explored this other facet of who I was.

The queer community I eventually found replaced or mirrored the large, welcoming, and joyful Indian community I'd grown up with, except that the new community was almost exclusively white. They knew a thing or two about identity construction, though; many of them had been forced to leave behind much of what they'd learned in their families, and several of them were exploring their own gender identity and expression. Some of them had changed names, discovered just how queer they could safely be at work, found or created evening and weekend spaces to use for refuge and recovery. From them, I learned that defining your worth on your own terms is wearying: forging your own identity, learning not to care, separating and disentangling, establishing the rules for your own life. Being queer cannot be taken up at a leisurely pace, put off for a time that seems more convenient; unlike the long arc that my Indian identity traced through my life, my post-coming-out queer identity felt more like an explosion that then required me to tinker with the pieces before they would fit back together.

Still, I did not know how to reconcile the world I'd been allowed into, a world in which I learned to reclaim the term "dyke" and think of my own gender expression as performative, with the brown world in which I'd been raised. I wanted to be able to honor the Indian part of my identity without feeling like a sellout, wanted to be able to own up to the parts of that identity that still felt authentic to me. In the wake of my dad's death, I decided to try to find a way to feel at home being Indian while also feeling at home being queer, no longer compartmentalizing the two.

In many cultures, grief comes with a change in appearance: traditions like wearing certain colors and clothes, rending garments, or shearing hair. For me to have cut my hair after my father died, though, would have been no change—I'd kept it short for years. So instead, I did two things my father had always wanted me to do: I grew my hair out, and I got my ears pierced. When I was younger, short hair and a lack of earrings had been markers of rebellion, ways to distinguish myself from "all the other" Indian girls I knew; suddenly, they became a demonstration of my desire to acknowledge my connection to my father's culture.

In India, as in many cultures, it is traditional to pierce a baby girl's ears in infancy. My mother didn't hold with this, however—she wanted me to be able to consent. So while all the brown girls I knew had their ears pierced from day one and the white girls I went to school with all waited anxiously for whichever birthday their parents had set as the boundary line for earrings, I kept my ears unpierced until I was twenty-four, a year after my father had died. Piercing my ears felt like the perfect way to mark my body, to look on the outside like the "good Indian girl" I'd always felt wary of being. The difference now, though, was that while I was wearing sets of earrings from my mom's literal dowry, and learning to put saris on by myself (with the help of YouTube), I was also finally out to everyone in my life, no longer keeping Jill a secret, no longer feeling quite so compartmentalized.

The "wearing a bindi every day" came next, and unexpectedly. I was in my first year of teaching, at a Jewish school, where I witnessed for the first time a very different approach to minority identity. Whereas I attended a school with very few students who shared my background, most of my students had spent their entire lives attending Jewish schools, participating in Jewish youth groups, and going to Jewish summer camps. Though they knew the outside world considered them "other," most of them had little direct experience with feeling that way.

I envied them. There was so much safety and celebration in their identity, which they didn't have to reserve only for the weekends or keep contained within their home. They didn't seem to know how good they had it; they complained about having to take Hebrew and Judaic studies, while I would have given anything to have had access to classes on Hindi and religions of India in high school. As I got to know my students' families, I noticed similar sets of generational tension around issues of assimilation and tradition, tensions I was intimately familiar with. Parents and grandparents struggled when religion didn't seem as important to their kids as it had been to them, insisting on bar and bat mitzvahs but wondering if the ritual had become too much about the party and not enough about the *parsha* (Torah portion); they felt relief that their children and grandchildren did not face the same type of open hostility and institutional anti-Semitism that they had but also worried that young people wouldn't be as committed to their Jewish identity if they didn't have to fight for it.

Halfway through my first year of teaching, I was asked to speak to the middle school student body about Hinduism during our morning assembly. Having attended an Episcopal school for twelve years, I was already practiced at being the religious minority in school spaces. Recalling the chapel talks I had given as a student, I pulled out some Indian clothes and a bindi for maximum impact. In my presentation, I attempted to explain or contextualize things I felt the students were most likely to encounter or be exposed to about Hinduism: images of gods and goddesses (especially Ganesh, whom everyone always has lots of questions about), the story behind the holiday of Diwali, the meaning of the om symbol, and the significance of a bindi.

After going through the most basic of the basics, I opened things up for questions. An eighth grader, not my student but a kid with whom I was friendly, raised his hand and asked me, "Ms. Mehra, if the bindi means all of those things, why don't you wear it all the time?"

I had compared the bindi with the Star of David many students opted to wear around their necks or on rings around their fingers: a marker of identity, of belonging, a way of saying *I am part of this tribe*. I had also explained the significance of the placement—symbolic of the third eye of Lord Shiva, seat of meditation and concentration. A reminder to be plugged in and present. I'd sold it well. No wonder he asked.

It was the first but most certainly not the last time I would say to a student, "You know, that's a really great question. And I'm not sure what the answer is." I probably *did* know the answer somewhere, deep down. But it was too embarrassing to admit to a room full of middle school students and my new colleagues. The truth was, to wear a bindi every day felt too brazen, too "out there." It would mean a more intense claim of my identity than I'd ever felt comfortable with before. My long hair and pierced ears meant something very personal, without necessarily being signifiers to anyone else. If I was to start wearing a bindi, I would be marking myself plainly, indicating who I was (at least to those who knew what a bindi was or meant). I'd be immediately identifiable to other members of my tribe.

———

Being first-generation and queer makes for quite a potent mix of desires and expectations. Growing up, I had the sense that I was constantly being held up to different sets of standards but found lacking on both sides. I wanted to be accepted by the dominant culture but also wanted to find my footing inside my minority identity—that was one juggling act. Once I had some facility with it, I found myself faced with the task of reconciling my queerness with all of the work I'd already done, a seemingly impossible task.

For a long time, I coped by distancing myself from Indian people other than the ones I had grown up with. Because I was self-conscious about whether I was "Indian enough," I was certain that others would judge me, too, would check to see if I lived up to their standard. My belief, based on stereotypes, was that I wouldn't; I was an unmarried liberal arts major who didn't speak Hindi but who did have a white girlfriend. It was one thing to be judged by white people—that was unavoidable—but I could avoid judgment by Indians if I simply kept out of their company. In college, I showed no interest in joining the South Asian Society and went to visit a local Hindu temple only once; it made me so uncomfortable that I never went back. (By way of contrast, I attended services at the Episcopal church across the street several times.) When I needed ingredients from the Indian grocery store, I'd send Jill, because no one there would expect *her* to speak Hindi.

I avoided overtures of friendship from other Indians, resented the implication that there should be some sort of automatic kinship between us, convinced myself that I "wasn't like them." I was the only Indian kid in my college and grad school friend groups, and I enjoyed and became accustomed to that experience. Irrationally, I felt that other people who shared my background might clue everyone else in to the fact that I was, as it turned out, a minority.

Over time, as I've grown more comfortable in my own

self-conception, I've grown more at ease—or, at least, less on edge—while in the company of other people who are brown like me. I can now see with some critical distance the ways in which I fell prey to the very stereotypes I thought I was trying to avoid; I didn't want to be "too Indian," and the American cultural imagination of my youth had a very fixed and rigid definition of what "Indian" looked like or meant, a definition that some Indians themselves share. The choice was either be that kid or resist being that kid.

But I wanted to have it both ways; I still do. I wear a bindi, eat beef, sleep with a white woman, throw a killer Diwali party, cannot resist Christmas music, and am snobby about mangoes, chai, cornbread, and pork barbecue. The term "desire lines" comes from architecture, referring to the natural paths created over time when enough people take an alternate route; think of college quads and the lines that cut diagonally across the grass, offering a quicker way to, say, the library than the ninety-degree turns a concrete sidewalk can provide. Feminist theorist Sara Ahmed sees desire lines as a way of "queering" a space, of changing the game. The presence of a desire line means that there is a different way of doing things; desire lines literally break new ground, creating physical proof of the pre-prescribed way not being the only way. For a long time, I thought I had to pick one sidewalk or another. Now I see that by claiming what feels authentic to me, I have made my own pathway in the grass.

I used to think that an inevitable part of occupying multiple identity categories was always feeling like something was missing. These days, I wonder if that's just another old way of seeing that requires rethinking. Instead of not being Indian enough or not being American enough or not being queer enough, what I have is a series of choices that results in me. I think about my son, who has an even broader set of choices than I did. After all, he has one mother who wears a bindi every day and one mother who duck hunts. He participates in *puja* with me and my mom and has learned to say "Bless this food in Jesus's name, amen" from his grandfather, Jill's dad. In both cases, Shiv improvises his four-year-old add-ons of gratitude: "Thank you for the trees and the birds and God and chocolate cake, amen."

Shiv, even more so than me, really raises the question *Who counts?* I'm Indian, but primarily by virtue of my genetics; both of my parents were from India. I'm southern, but only by the virtue of my geography; I was born and then raised in Memphis, Tennessee. Technically, Shiv is second-generation, and in the classic narrative of immigrant life, the second generation moves further away from the culture of origin, assimilating to a degree beyond what was possible for their first-generation parents. But will this be true of Shiv? Like me, he is American by birth; unlike me, he is not ethnically Indian. Still, he is my child, and he is his grandmother's grandson—will he feel like he is second-generation? Will he experience himself as Indian or having ties to an Indian heritage? He has been exposed to and participated in Indian cultural practices since he was born, and Hinduism is the dominant religious framework of his childhood. (Though Jill's parents are observant Christians, Jill is not.) He's obsessed with Hindu mythology and prefers reading it to the Bible we have a copy of. (Recently, when looking at a book about Vikings and seeing the stone renderings of their gods, he told me, "Our gods are much more beautiful-er than their gods, Mama.") He's eaten Indian food his whole life, celebrated Hindu holidays, and understands Hindi perfectly because my mother speaks to him in it exclusively, at my request.

The identity categories that Shiv embodies make sense to him and make sense to us, his family; they seem natural, obvious. But taken outside the scope of our family, they can begin to be puzzling. When he grows older, will he have trouble gaining access to Indian culture and experiences? Will he want that access? Will he have to prove he belongs? And what of his blackness? Everything that is housed inside of his lived experience, will it help expand our collective imagination about what black life can look like, or will it instead block him from belonging when others don't recognize him? Shiv calls everything into question.

Sometimes it feels like I'm still on the identity seesaw, though not as often as it used to. But the feeling inevitably creeps in—here I am, being a good Indian girl by keeping vegetarian during a Hindu holy week, but being a bad southern guest when I have to turn down homemade ribs to do so. I feel like I've earned a southern cook merit badge when I cure my own ham for Easter, then like a slacker Indian parent when I realize that my son has not yet celebrated Holi. It helps, though, that there are more and more models for this kind of life, more demonstrations of hybridity and creativity—instead of feeling guilt for defaulting to Christian hymns when my son asks for a song at bedtime, I am working to embrace it, to acknowledge that "Seek Ye First" is deeply embedded in my consciousness, and that's okay. There's nothing wrong or bad with being someone most people haven't seen the likes of before.

I wonder what will linger for Shiv when he is old enough to make his own choices. The ethos I want to pass on to him when it comes to collaging one's identity is this: Keep things slippery. Embrace your desire lines and don't let anyone force you to make an accounting for them. They'll want to define or capture you—don't let them. You don't need to help them make sense of you, as long as you make sense to yourself.

Cult of Motherhood

I have always known that I wanted to be a parent: no doubts, no uncertainty, no "depends on who I end up with," no question. I was going to be a mama one way or another. In high school, I became convinced that I wouldn't wind up partnered until much later in life (I was a late bloomer), so I told my parents to be prepared for me to adopt as a single mom when I turned thirty. Then, when I was nineteen, I met the woman who would become my wife, shifting that narrative dramatically. Another shift: Jill was thirty-eight, had already decided not to have kids, and had built a life for herself without children. Then I became a part of that life, bringing along my fervent desire to parent. What had seemed like a certainty to me for so long morphed more and more into a question.

I'd always thought I would have a baby the way most women do: by getting pregnant. My own mother worked hard to make pregnancy happen for her; it took many years, a great deal of heartache, and not a small amount of money. The story of how I came to be and the attendant determination that brought me into the world have long framed my understanding of parenthood as something undertaken with solemnity and effort.

These days, in my professional and social circle, parenthood is a default choice, a matter of course, part of the plan. Perhaps this is more prevalent in the South, or in immigrant communities, but the experience of childless women in my life is that they are constantly being called to account for, even challenged on, the reason they don't have kids. I half tease, half scold my own mom for acting like "such an Indian grandmother" when she asks me when my recently married friends are going to have kids. Thankfully, she knows better than to ask my recently married friends themselves. One of my colleagues got bombarded in the reception line at her wedding by a brand-new in-law: "So, when are you two going to start a family?" I have my own baggage about the assumption that two people in a committed relationship don't constitute a family; Jill and I experienced plenty of that as a couple who couldn't legally marry until thirteen years into our relationship. But even we have been subject to a second set of questions, which arrive like clockwork around the time your first child turns one: *When are you going to have another? Don't you want to give your child a sibling?*

For certain people in my life—colleagues who are Orthodox Jews and friends who are Evangelical Christians—the reasons for having children are clearly articulated within their religious tradition. But for the rest of us, science has proved that having kids doesn't make you happy—in fact, it tends to make most people unhappier—and it isn't particularly good for your marriage, if you have one. Raising kids limits you financially, impacts your ability to capitalize on all kinds of opportunities, and, if you're a woman, can screw up your body and be detrimental to your career. So why do it?

I know couples who wish they'd waited longer to have kids; who wish they'd had only one instead of two; who even feel that, as much as they love their children, they should have given more thought to whether they should have become parents in the first place. Suggestion and socialization are powerful, and my lay-person's knowledge of biology helps me understand how force-fully our bodies can push us to do things that are not rational or in our own self-interest. For all of the conversations about *how* to parent, the debates over styles and approaches, the millions of dollars of marketing devoted to convincing parents of the neces-sity of one baby registry item or another, we fail to discuss whether someone's choice to parent in the first place is a good idea.

Parenting may well be the life experience around which we have the most expectation, which is why I find it puzzling that there is such a lack of discussion around entering into it. Though there is more room now, culturally, for women to express their reasons for choosing not to parent, men seem not to need to explain why they don't want to have kids. Middle- and upper-middle-class adults view having kids as an inevitability; there is no conversa-tion and little coaching (where's the premarital counseling equiv-alent for child-rearing?) around deciding "whether or not," because the question has already been answered.

When you're in a relationship like mine, there's absolutely zero chance anyone will get pregnant by accident, so having a child nec-essarily becomes a deliberate undertaking. In my early twenties, there were times when I worried—despaired, even—that I would have to leave my relationship with Jill in order to become a par-ent. I respected, tremendously, the fact that she was unwilling to tackle parenting with anything less than a full commitment; I wasn't interested in jumping into parenthood with someone who wasn't totally on board. But I couldn't imagine a life for myself without a child, or without Jill.

Then in late 2004, Jill opened up the paper and read an account of AIDS orphans in Africa. Along with the newspaper story was a picture of an orphan—Bruno—no more than two or three years old, clinging to the legs of an aid worker. All of the boy's relatives were dead. Jill, deeply moved by this story, began to think differently about the prospect of becoming a parent. She felt herself drawn powerfully to the prospect of adoption, which we had tossed around as an option but not seriously considered or investigated. In the end, it was Jill's compassion and deeply embedded sense of ethics—her desire to step in where others couldn't—that led to us deciding officially to become parents and to do so through adoption.

In this way, my narrative about parenting moved away from sperm donors and pregnancy and birth toward a new image of what becoming a mother might look like. The transition was not difficult; I was not as attached as I thought I might be to biological parenting, to the thread of genetics or the experience of carrying a child inside my body. Choosing adoption pushed me to think about what exactly I was attached to and why.

For most couples, adoption is plan B; they come to adoption after trying, unsuccessfully, to conceive. For this reason, agencies stress the importance of distinguishing between the need to have a baby and the need to become a parent. Though our culture conflates the two, they are not the same thing. My attachment to having a baby was not nearly as strong as my desire to become a parent, which made moving into adoption a fairly joyful choice. Many couples who have struggled with infertility are able to make the same choice, although they may simultaneously experience deep grief over the prospect of not having a baby. But I've read accounts from others, both single prospective parents and couples, for whom getting pregnant and giving birth are essential and not something they're willing to give up on. The language of possessives runs consistently through the accounts of these stories, references to a child "of my own," "of our own," "of their own."

There is still a widespread feeling that adopted children are somehow less connected to their parents than biological children. Jill and I are the only adoptive couple we know who didn't try to make a baby either before adopting or after. There are others like us, but as far as I can tell, we're in the minority. Because of this, I catch myself internally questioning couples who spend so much time and energy trying to conceive and carry a biological child. I know this is unfair; just because it wasn't hard for me to give up my own attachment to conceiving and giving birth to a child doesn't mean it is that easy for others. I may not understand why some people possess such a strong need to have a baby, but I don't have to. Adoption is not for everyone, and while I'd like to see more people consider it, my response stems more from how difficult it can be to live in a culture that conceives of parenthood, especially motherhood, as being inextricably and exclusively tied to biology. Biology is the primary lens through which motherhood is examined, translated, and evaluated. It is the be-all and end-all, the complete justification for parenting behavior and choices, which is why I've seen people balk at the cost of adoption while at the same time seeming to understand perfectly why prospective parents would spend the same amount of money (and in some cases more) to pursue fertility treatments.

My parents considered adoption toward the end of their fertility struggle, right before conceiving me. My mother was willing—like me, she always knew she wanted to become a parent—but my father was wary. He worried that he would not be able to fully love or love in the same way a child whom he adopted, a child that wasn't "his." My mom didn't understand this feeling; she worked as a special ed teacher for nearly forty years, in classrooms full of infants and toddlers. Long before she became a parent, she had fallen in love with dozens of children that "weren't hers."

What's more, my mom has never been particularly close to her own biological family, with the exception of her brother. I'm in a similar boat; other than my parents, my experience with "blood family" is extremely limited. I've spent my entire life on a continent where the only people related to me were my two parents. My only tie to dozens of family members in India is through my parents. I love those relatives in theory, but I don't really know them. A few awkward phone calls (now emails or Facebook messages) a year coupled with three visits to India have generated affection but not closeness. The people who feel like my "real" family are the ones my parents raised me with, fellow Indian immigrants and their first-generation kids, "uncles" and "aunties" who aren't related to me at all but with whom I share history. In my experience, blood has never been a prerequisite for bonding.

While I felt some loss at the prospect of missing out on an experience I'd envisioned for so long, I realized that essentially what I would be missing was the experience of doing things "like everyone else." My fantasies related to pregnancy had been wholly aesthetic: how I would look, how people would respond to me, the things I would buy and wear, all the material shifts in my being and our life. None of these concerns dealt directly with the actual child I'd be giving birth to or changed the fact that, ultimately, the end result would be the same—I would become a parent.

When you tell people that you've adopted, or are planning to adopt, they tend to respond with gushy enthusiasm. "Oh, that's so *great* of you!" as if you just donated money to charity or gave blood. People mean well, but their ability to respond in a useful or meaningful way has been short-circuited by Hollywood dramas and British children's books about orphans, which is why the conventional narrative about adoption is transactional and incomplete. The implication is that adoption is a sad but necessary societal structure, a tragic yet noble experience undertaken only by desperate people.

Everyone knows what to say when you announce that you're pregnant, but adoption is different. It's like its own mysterious, subterranean world: when you enter into it, you disappear from view. Friends and family don't know how to comment on your experience the way they would if you were four or six or eight months pregnant; they don't know what questions to ask, and most of the questions they do ask are unhelpful.

So much of the predictable "chatter" around babies has to do with speculation around who that baby will look like and whose mannerisms the infant will inherit, but none of that works when you're adopting. Even a baby shower can be a tricky matter; some adoptive parents match with a birth mother at five months, others get a phone call once the baby has been born. While expectant parents are sent on "babymoons" and spend their weekends "nesting" in the baby's room, if you're waiting to hear from an adoption agency, you're advised to hold off on decorating or acquiring too much baby stuff—should the adoption fall through, these things serve only as painful reminders.

Because most people have little knowledge of what the experience of adopting is like, they tend to comment on it by contrasting it to what they *do* know. I had more than one woman comment that I was "skipping the hard part," a statement that might have been devastating had I been someone who'd struggled with infertility, but one that also managed to elevate the work of biology while discounting the effort that goes into adoption, not to mention the work of actual parenting once a baby is born. To undertake a comparison is inane—I'm not interested in participating in some kind of suffering Olympics—but much of what is challenging about adoption is its invisibility. Due to the unpredictable nature of the process, the decision to adopt is often kept secret for many months. You are expecting a child, yes, but no one looks at your belly and smiles or provides you with special parking at the grocery store. No one sees the small mountain of paperwork you've filled out: medical forms, financial documents, recommendation letters, floor plans of your living space, FBI background checks. Other parents do not have to engage with the Autobiographical Instrument, a fifteen-page document that our agency required both of us to fill out, full of questions like *What was the biggest disappointment or loss you have experienced in your life and how did you cope with it? Describe yourself as a marital partner, including both your strengths and weaknesses.* On my least charitable days, I resented being put through such a rigorous discernment prospect when seemingly everyone around me was managing to have babies without their fitness as parents being questioned.

For Jill and me, adoption also revealed the extent to which most of our straight friends were out of touch with the reality of what it meant for us to be a same-sex couple. They seemed to assume that simply wanting a baby would be enough to qualify us to get one, but as two women living in Texas, Jill and I had to tread carefully. Our refusal to pretend to be "roommates" in the pre-*Obergefell* era led us to choose private adoption over public, but nearly all private adoption agencies are religiously affiliated, meaning almost exclusively Christian. Even nondenominational agencies can have incredibly narrow sets of qualifications for adoptive parents, including age, marital status, and health history. As a couple who could not yet legally marry, we were out of luck almost everywhere, and even though we found a wonderful agency that welcomed us, we still—because of the law—had to apply to adopt separately, which meant a longer, more expensive, and emotionally fraught process.

Conventional narratives about adoption tend to focus on the adoptive parents, holding them up as heroes or rescuers, highlighting how much they "deserve" to be parents; birth mothers are either pitied or judged, the fullness of their stories and circumstances mostly ignored. It took me some time to realize that I, too, was entering into the adoption process with an incomplete narrative at work. My focus was on Jill and me, on our experience, on what *we* wanted; mainly, I wanted the process to be easy.

For this reason, I resisted at first the partially open adoption process that our agency, like most these days, utilizes. "Partially open" means that birth parents and adoptive parents meet before the baby is born, that adoptive parents have access to medical information and paperwork, and that birth parents have the right to receive updates and pictures at least once a year. Though intellectually I supported the fact that the transactional, anonymous procedure of the old days was, for the most part, no longer in practice, the new way sounded harder. The thought of meeting with a birth mother, seeing her and speaking with her, reminded me that I was not becoming a parent the "normal" way. It reminded me of the complication and messiness. Reminded me that this wasn't simply about my lifelong desire to become a parent, but that there were real people at the center of this circle—namely a birth mother and the child we would share.

June 2012: I am in the kitchen at a friend's house, about to give an informal Indian food cooking lesson. After taking my phone from my pocket, I scroll through my email quickly, planning to put my phone away for the next couple of hours. Instead, I read an email from our adoption agency, telling me that a birth mother has expressed interest in meeting Jill and me. She is nearly eight months pregnant.

After several jubilant phone calls and a fair amount of crying, I still manage to teach my friends how to make *bhindi masala*. Jill is out of town (though she makes plans to return quickly), so we conference call with our birth mother that night. I am standing on the rug in the middle of our living room, too nervous to sit down, and in the darkening light I hear an unfamiliar voice come through the phone and it's as if time stops. What do you say to a person who is considering giving you their child? How do you make small talk with a stranger with whom you will be inextricably linked for the rest of your life?

We learn that she's been having bad heartburn, which means the baby probably has a lot of hair. She's having trouble sleeping, can't get comfortable in the bed, and has been craving barbacoa tacos and Dr Pepper. She's excited to meet us in a few days, at a lunch date that the agency has arranged. We tell her we've been referring to our someday-baby as "Peanut." She likes that. She will refer to him that way exclusively for the following year, until she falls out of touch.

Our son is born seventeen days after we meet his birth mother for lunch at a Tex-Mex restaurant, the most awkward and intimate meal of my life. Over the course of those days, she is incredibly generous with us, permitting us to remain in the hospital delivery room with her as Shiv comes sailing out of her body.

There is a natural limit to the number of compliments that can be afforded newborns; contrary to what parents may think, most of them look swollen and terrible. Babies can't do much of anything, so there's no real opportunity to comment on their abilities, which means that well-wishers tend to connect the child back to their parents in their congratulatory remarks: "He's got your nose!" or, "She's beautiful, like her mama!"—even if these are a stretch, they seem to bring some comfort, some assurance. But they were inapplicable to us.

Well past Shiv's birth, my family and its dimensions continue to bring to light how much of the language we use to speak about parenting and families is premised on one specific type of family, or an imitation of that type of family. Think of the maternal threat *I brought you into this world and I can take you out of it!* Or of the power that the possessive pronoun confers; *I want to have your baby* is seductive and alluring in a way that *I want to have a baby* is not.

Everywhere, the language of parenting, and especially motherhood, excludes my family; even those who ought to know better often don't. At my last appointment, my OB-GYN had to catch and correct herself midsentence: "Women who haven't had children— I mean, who haven't given birth . . ." Friends will use the term "real parents" when they mean "birth parents," then see the involuntary look of hurt on my face and stumble. A coworker seemed disappointed when she learned that I had adopted Shiv, whom she'd met when I brought him to school. "Oh," she said, "I thought he was yours."

Sometimes people will try to impose a sense of biological belonging on our family experience, revealing the extent to which our collective vocabulary remains limited. "I swear, Nishta and Shiv have the same smile!" or, "Look at how Jill and Shiv have the same cheeks!" These remarks are intended as compliments, but they are also silly. Shiv does not look like either of us, nor does he need to for us to be fully "his" parents and for him to be fully "our" child. Even Shiv himself, though he knows perfectly well the story of his birth and adoption, will sometimes ask, "Was that when I was in your tummy?" because that narrative is so pervasive and all-encompassing.

As frustrating as these moments of incongruence are, there are times when it is undeniably tempting to give in to the dominant narrative, to try to make our story fit with everyone else's. My first experience of this came with breastfeeding, so often the battleground for moms these days; for me, though, it was a personal experience that both set me apart and allowed me access to the mainstream.

Almost immediately after we matched with Shiv's birth mother, I began to try to induce lactation, which not a lot of people know you can even do. With the help of medicine and a whole lot of pumping using a rented hospital-grade machine, I was able to produce tiny amounts of milk just a few days before Shiv was born. Once he began nursing, my supply increased, but we continued to supplement with donated milk and formula.

I'm not going to lie—successfully inducing lactation made me feel like a total badass. Though I know it wasn't a reflection on my inner virtue or even my fitness as a parent, there were times when others implied this and I didn't correct them. Shiv was "so lucky" to have a mother who would go through all of this trouble to feed him; in the eyes of militant breastfeeding advocates, I was a living reproach to mothers who "gave up" on breastfeeding or who chose formula outright, heaven forbid.

I don't regret nursing Shiv, but I do feel a little bit complicit each time I "talk shop" with breastfeeding colleagues. As I am unable to discuss or relate to the experience of pregnancy or giving birth, it's so *nice* to be able to join in on a conversation about how awful it is to pump at work. Jumping into those conversations often requires some explanation, which serves only to draw more attention to my own story.

Drawing this attention is not all bad—it helps to open up people's understanding of what breastfeeding can look like and who can be a part of that club, while also sharing a bit about the singularity of the experience for us "hidden" members. Indeed, this is what I'd like to see more of overall: a way to honor the fact that my experience as someone who became a parent through adoption is, in many ways, different. I would like my experience to be included in the broader conversation. I would like there to be more room to depict underrepresented experiences not as novelties to be gawked at but as honest narratives that might help expand our collective imagination around the work of parenting. I want there to be more room for what palliative care physician B. J. Miller refers to as the "strange beauty" of human experience.

I thought becoming a parent was the tricky part, but what I failed to realize was how fraught the identity politics of motherhood are once you've brought your baby home. Every choice is polarizing, throwing you into one camp or another: co-sleeping or crib, on-demand feeding or scheduled. When Shiv was born, I was completely unprepared for the way that our parenting choices, made inside of private, thoughtful conversations, would prove divisive to the point that it affected relationships with friends. We are people who cast a fairly wide net when it comes to friendships; we socialize with people who hold different political and religious convictions from ours, who have different ethnic and socioeconomic backgrounds, but parenting style is the one dividing line we can't seem to bridge. Differences in opinion are inevitably seen as condemnation of the other. To even talk about our choices seemed to register as an assault to friends making different ones.

Jill and I were also unprepared for the extent to which we were expected to change after becoming parents. All around us was this assumption that motherhood would now become our primary identity, that it must naturally and necessarily have overtaken all other facets of our identity. "You know how you go out to dinner but all you end up talking about is the baby?" The first time a girlfriend said this to me, I realized that I was supposed to nod along in agreement even though it wasn't true for me and Jill, even though the thought that I would suddenly be unable to talk to my spouse about anything other than our child, when we had spent a decade before his birth engaging in all kinds of topics, was incredibly disturbing.

Even though I am a person with a child, I resent the implications made about what parenthood (particularly motherhood) is or isn't and what it does or doesn't mean; not only does it leave a lot of people out, it also insults other women and limits us. We reinforce the same stereotypes about ourselves that we say we want to break. Childless friends vent their frustration at motherhood being wielded as a kind of impunity, an inarguable excuse for any and all behaviors that might otherwise be seen as rude or inconsiderate. If you don't have kids, you can't possibly understand, and you're not allowed to disagree or judge.

In our cult of motherhood, we ignore all the work that's done in support of parents, work that makes parenting possible, work parents can't do that others tackle. Colleagues volunteer to cover a class so that I can leave school for my son's doctor appointment; Shiv's grandmother provides child care that allows Jill and me to spend time alone together without having to pay for a babysitter. As a teacher, I know that my son's teachers see and understand him in ways that I never will, and I know that they provide care and instruction he needs but can't get from me. Shiv's "aunties" and "uncles," our friends who have adopted him into their own lives, provide essential love, nurturing, and relationships. In fact, it is primarily the aunties and uncles who are themselves not parents, or whose children are grown, who have the energy left to give to my son. This work is often invisible or erased, all credit going to the parents.

When I voice my dissent or fail to chime in on the chorus, I sometimes hear remarks along the lines of *It must be because you didn't give birth to him.* The implication is that I don't love my son as much as "real" parents love theirs, or else I'd see their parenting choices as the correct ones and adopt them myself. And the truth is that many of the choices Jill and I make do relate to the fact that we didn't give birth to Shiv—we are careful not to think about him as "ours." There is a kind of freedom in the adoptive experience, a reminder that our children do not belong to us. Shiv's autonomy has been paramount from the start; he is a separate being, with his own will. We are responsible for him, but we do not control him.

When I see other parents planning their children's futures, invested in certain outcomes (playing this sport, entering this profession, going to this college), I am reminded of my own experience of parental expectations as the first-generation daughter of immigrants. Growing up, I was acutely aware that I served as living proof of my parents' competence and worthiness. I felt duty bound to produce a certain kind of success in order to reflect well on them, a scheme that exploded in all of our faces when it turned out I was queer. Now that I am raising my own child, I am deeply invested in not re-creating that kind of pressure for him. I have several avenues of identity through which I realize my self-worth; parenting is a role I take very seriously, but it is far from the only thing that matters to me. Redefining motherhood includes expanding our cultural idea of what it means for a woman to be a parent. The author and activist Rebecca Solnit has written that our society perceives motherhood as "the key to feminine identity," ignoring the fact that "there are so many things to love besides one's own offspring, so many things that need love, so much other work love has to do in the world." If we can expand beyond our notion that parenting is somehow mysteriously intuitive, effortless, and necessary for women to live full and meaningful lives, we could give all women more credit for the various kinds of work they choose to do in the world.

The Sin of Our Security

Yesterday, I sat with my wife and two friends as our boys frolicked in a neighborhood kids' pool. Though it's less than two feet at its deepest point, the primary appeal of the wading pool is its large play structure, with stairs, slides, and falling buckets of water; this creates the perfect environment for play-pretend, chasing, and splashing. There were a handful of other kids in the pool, including a little boy who appeared to be about five years old. He kept mostly to himself and didn't draw my attention until he attempted to go down the slide hands first, Superman style, the way all of the other kids his size were doing. At this, his parents—who were sitting nearby—freaked out, both of them yelling at him until he flipped himself around. After he came down the slide "correctly," they pulled him out of the pool for a stern talk. "If you do that again, we're going home!"

My wife and our friends raised our eyebrows at one another, puzzled by what seemed like a disproportionate response to not particularly dangerous behavior. For one, this kid was wearing goggles and a Puddle Jumper (a flotation device that fits around the arms and chest). What's more, the slide in question sloped gently and stood no more than four feet tall; it dumped kids out into about six inches of water, where a foam mat was affixed to the bottom of the pool to cushion landings. If all that weren't enough to ensure safety, a lifeguard was stationed at the edge of the pool the entire time.

This is the core irony I've encountered by parenting within a middle- to upper-middle-class, fairly racially diverse, suburban milieu: the amount of fear present is disproportionate to the amount of actual danger. Most, but not all, of the parents Jill and I encounter are frenetic, obsessive, and overprotective. So when we find ones who aren't, we befriend and cling to them like islands of sanity.

If I sound judgmental, it's because I am—helicopter (or, as Jill calls them, "hovercraft") parents drive me nuts. But worse than the parents themselves is the way the broader culture jokingly excuses their intense behavior, acknowledging that it is excessive and annoying but also insisting that it's understandable—*it's because they love their kids so much!* Except I don't believe that it's love driving the need to eliminate all potential dangers and alleviate all harm for one's child; I believe it's control—or rather the desire for control—that does.

We live in a society that hungers for security: airport security, online security, financial security, job security. In a 2015 podcast interview, Simone Campbell, nun, lawyer, and lobbyist, diagnosed our cultural mood: "I think our sin is our obsession with security. Our obsession that everything ought to work out perfectly for us . . . this obsession with having everything we need." The word "sin" is one I traditionally eschew, for all kinds of reasons related both to my personal religious background and to my queerness, but here I find it extremely compelling. To sin is to transgress; but theologically, the meaning goes even further—to sin is to be separate from God. In the Western myth of the Garden of Eden, when sin first enters the picture, Adam and Eve's punishment is to be sent away—they are estranged. I would argue that our obsession with security is likewise the result of estrangement: not necessarily from God (that's not my argument to make) but from reality, the natural way of things, the truth of how the world works.

I grew up well protected; my parents didn't baby me, but they didn't exactly encourage adventurousness either. Many of the things considered formative and character building by white Americans didn't make sense to my immigrant parents. We never went camping, for instance: the appeal of sleeping on the ground did not translate across cultures. Daring feats of physical exertion were also puzzling—no skiing, no marathon running—as one of the status privileges of becoming a "have" as opposed to a "have not" was not needing to use your body to make your living. Badminton, gardening, and walking were the only physical activities I ever saw my parents participate in. The only summer camp I ever attended was "nerd camp," the Talent Identification Program at Duke University that requires a qualifying SAT score for admission and includes daily academic classes instead of lake swimming or archery. I had the earliest curfew of all my friends and there were many concerts and parties I wasn't allowed to go to. Though I was encouraged to be brave with my thoughts (for which I'll always be grateful), my parents cautioned me to play it safe with my body.

My mother is a worrier, a worst-case-scenario person. She has had a lot of difficult and hard things happen in her life: her mother died when she was two, her relationship with her father fell apart when she married my dad, and my parents struggled for nearly fifteen years to have a baby, enduring several miscarriages along the way. For her, the world is scary and dangerous—and to be fair, the world *is* scary and dangerous. But the world of my particular childhood bubble was not. In the grand scheme of things, and certainly compared with my parents' own upbringings, I was incredibly sheltered. I did not endure hardship. And when I look back at my childhood, I see a much more timid version of the person I am now. I did not care much for novelty or new experiences; they made me nervous. There are many things that I said "no" to that I now wish I had not. Throughout my adult life, I have worked hard to make myself more risk tolerant, to fight against my own need to be good at everything I do, my fear of getting hurt or embarrassing myself. I understand my mom's desire to protect me and I do not blame her for it. My parents were guided by a credo that many first-generation kids know by heart: *We want you to have a better life than we had.* But who defines "better"? And what do we sacrifice when we gain privilege and eschew hardship?

Privilege tends to breed entitlement. And entitlement—the sense "that everything ought to work out perfectly for us"—is a pathway through which we fool ourselves and our children into thinking that we are in control. Judgmental as I may be, I have to acknowledge my own participation in this form of thinking. After all, the whole premise of adoption is that adoptive parents can offer a child a better life than that child's birth parents. But again, who defines "better"? In our son's case, Jill and I give him a level of access afforded by economic privilege that his birth mother could not provide. But we still can't guarantee his safety, not any more or less than anyone else can. Herein lies the tension of parenting within privilege—while it makes sheltering possible, it also makes those sheltered children potentially less resilient and less prepared to cope with events that will inevitably challenge their privilege: sickness, death, heartache, frustration, failure. Everyone, no matter how much privilege they have, will someday have to reckon with what poet David Whyte calls in an interview the question of incarnation:

> *Being here in your body . . . the more you're here and the more you're alive, the more you realize you're a mortal human being . . . will you actually turn up? Will you become a full citizen of vulnerability, loss, and disappearance, which you have no choice about?*

When I was twenty-three, I watched my father go from seemingly healthy to completely incapacitated and on a ventilator in the course of two weeks. I went from living with no conscious thought of my father's mortality to signing a DNR and standing at his bedside while he died. That experience drove home every cliché I'd ever heard about how human beings have no guarantees yet live as if they do. I, too, had lived this way.

Five years later, my wife, Jill, was diagnosed with cancer. She was in her late forties, and only because she pinched a nerve in her neck did doctors discover the shadowy mass beneath her breastbone. Like my father, she went from perfectly healthy to completely vulnerable, her body wrecked first by chemo, then open-chest surgery. Unlike my father, she survived. But in the time of uncertainty that her illness brought, the fear that is always lurking around the edges of life was invited into the center of our relationship, shared our intimate space. The work, we learned, was neither to ignore that fear nor to let it take over. And though the immediacy of that fear receded when Jill's doctor proclaimed her "cancer free," we have continued to live with the knowledge that it could return at any time, in ways we can never predict, and for no reason at all.

Affluent twenty-first-century parents seem to believe that if we just find the right parenting blog or book, or buy the correct swaddling blanket and diffuse properly sourced essential oils, we can guarantee our children's happiness and well-being. All around me, parenting looks like following your children around on the playground in case they fall or need help, paying a professional baby-proofing service to round each sharp corner in your house, cutting grapes in half, and covering your kid in safety gear to ride a tricycle that stands less than two feet off the ground. In a *Time* magazine editorial, actress Jemima Kirke referred to this as a "culture of overprotective methodology and vigilance" that "makes us believe that if we do things correctly, if we have all the information, we'll be safe and our children will be safe."

This mind-set also means taking credit when what we do seems to work, as I did when Shiv was a baby. Being an adoptive parent, I feel myself cheerleading for team Nurture, wanting to affirm the work Jill and I did as parents and the choices that we made. Shiv took to a schedule well, slept through the night at three and a half months, ate everything we fed him, loved reading books. He was not fussy, never demonstrated stranger anxiety—he was what other parents called an "easy baby." But how much of that temperament came with him and how much of it was encouraged by us? It's easy to feel superior and become judgmental of others when you have a baby like that, though I'm quick to switch allegiance to team Nature, when it comes to Shiv's temper; his outbursts of anger and frustration can be made to fit into a narrative that would mirror what little we know about his birth father's temperament. Of course, we'll never be able to sort all this out definitively, and that's not even the point. What my camp switching reveals is how eager I am to tell a story in which *I* am the one responsible for my child's fate—a figure who is necessary, needed, the one in control. In doing this, I ignore the fact that at the most basic level, the world is dangerous and unpredictable, and we humans are profoundly not in control.

Modern life does its best to fool us into thinking we *do* have control, particularly if we live with certain economic means. Our lives are full of choices—how many times have I stood, frozen in an aisle at Target, dazzled by just how many kinds of toothpaste are for sale?—and we are likewise encouraged to give our children choices, to encourage their autonomy and sense of self. We are planners and calendar keepers; we sign up for day care when our babies are still in utero, enroll them in elite private schools before they can form a sentence. Projecting into the future, we map out their lives decades in advance, fully expecting their success and our carefree days as blissed-out grandparents.

What's ironic is that while our money affords us physical security—safer neighborhoods, professions less demanding on the body, access to quality medical care—existentially, we are far removed from our status as mortal creatures. And to live so far removed from the inevitability of sickness and death is to become more vulnerable. We think we can control or limit the amount of difficulty that will come our way, which only makes us less equipped to deal when it does.

Even before I became a parent, I saw overprotective parenting play out in the classroom, where the concern is more about psychic than bodily harm. Working with seniors at a college prep school in an affluent part of Houston, I am intimately familiar with what nearly two decades' worth of protective parenting can look like. I see students terrified of failure, terrified of answering a question wrong, terrified that one step in the "wrong" direction will send their lives down a path of despair. They have been raised on a narrative that promises that if they do what's expected of them—curate the perfect college application, get into a "good" school so that they can have a "good" job—happiness will magically manifest.

By age sixteen or seventeen, they have, for the most part, debunked some of the myths they've been fed about happiness. At the same time, they have little practice with mystery and ambiguity; it makes them incredibly uncomfortable. They want clear answers, clean narratives. They want guarantees. They want to pick their college roommate the second they find out they've been admitted, utilizing camp friends and social media to help them match with someone they think they'll like, try as I might to convince them of the value of learning to live with someone you don't particularly like or who doesn't particularly like you.

As it turns out, the mystery and ambiguity of existence are not resolved when students make it to that dream college or move in with the painstakingly chosen roommate. (In fact, it's often the students who don't get into their dream school who end up thriving, as they are forced to make a reckoning between what they've been told to want and what they genuinely want, who they've been told to be and who they genuinely are.) Second-semester seniors get all of the blame for being unmotivated and entitled, but haven't we parents and educators reaped what we sowed? We talk out of two sides of our mouth, one proclaiming the gospel of learning for learning's sake and growth, creativity, and risk, but that side is quickly drowned out by the sound of the voice that pushes achievement and status and conformity and compliance and test scores and padded résumés. So I do not think we should be surprised when suddenly our college-bound seniors are not so sure what all of that work was for, cynical about the hoops they jumped through and parts of themselves they compromised. When they wonder a little bit about the bill of goods they've been sold and what else they've been fed that might also be bogus.

Not all my students were raised inside of a matrix that shelters them, nor do I place sole blame on parents for perpetuating the idea of a golden ladder that leads to happiness. As Rebecca Solnit puts it, "The idea that a life should seek meaning seldom emerges; not only are the standard activities assumed to be inherently meaningful, they are treated as the only meaningful options." So often, I find that students have not been asked what they care about, what they value, what kind of person they want to be. We do not encourage them to interrogate the standards of our society, preferring instead that they accept them as offered. Then, when the system fails them, they are left thinking it is they who failed.

Freshman year of college is hard for most people; I remember spending most of September and October of mine being terribly homesick. I was far from home on 9/11 and didn't know anyone well enough to hug. I had never spent so much time on my own. And yet, though I spent a lot of time alone, I didn't feel lonely. Though at times I was sad, I was not unhappy. I was learning a tremendous amount about myself, about my capabilities. A deep part of me knew that the only way out was through; I could feel myself growing and strengthening. As I emerged from the other side triumphant, I was deeply empowered by the fact that I'd figured out how to weather a difficult time. I knew the truth of what the poet Kahlil Gibran so famously said: "The deeper that sorrow carves into your being, the more joy you can contain."

Too often, Americans equate hard or sad with bad and wrong,

a feeling that we need to dispel. Our relentless obsession with happiness above all else—*I just want you to be happy!*—offers no tools for creating any kind of long-lasting meaning or satisfaction in our lives. As parents, we sometimes dismiss hurt when all it needs is to be acknowledged, given space. We tell our children not to cry, not because crying is bad for them but because it makes *us* uncomfortable. We want things to turn out okay, but to pretend that something will be okay when it clearly isn't is to make the classic parental mistake of issuing promises we can't keep. Sadness is a natural occurrence in any human life; surely it would be better to equip our children to cope with it than to push it away.

I came to resent this *I just want you to be happy / everything's going to be okay / don't be sad* mind-set when my father died. Grieving gave me a useful vantage point for observing how we, as a culture, deal with death—namely, we don't. Though I seemed to merit an extra layer of sympathy for losing a parent so young, about six weeks after my father's funeral, the default response of those around me was to resist or try to "fix" my grief. "I know you're sad right now, but you'll get back to your happy self again soon!" one well-meaning friend wrote.

Over time, I learned how to occupy my grief: not turning away from it, or folding into it, but sitting with it, letting it be. Grief is a project, but it works on you instead of you working on it. Theorist and researcher Pauline Boss talks about how American culture is one of "mastery orientation," meaning that our culture's orientation is toward solving problems, rendering us fairly ill equipped to handle questions that have no clear answer or problems that can't be solved. Death and grief represent a "kind of mystery . . . [that] gives us a feeling of helplessness that we're very uncomfortable with as a society." No wonder we're terribly ill equipped to deal with grief. There is courage required in not turning away, and doing so can feel radical when you're standing in the face of a culture and society that will accuse you of being morose and depressing and instead encourage you to "move on." To instead live life inside of ambiguity is to make room for a more complicated, messy kind of truth, what British Romantic poet John Keats called "negative capability": "the ability to contemplate the world without the desire to try and reconcile contradictory aspects or fit it into closed and rational systems." Living with unanswered questions and unknowable outcomes goes against our modern instincts.

"Unanswered questions and unknowable outcomes" could be a tagline for the adoption experience. Becoming an adoptive parent gave me a jump start on making peace with insecurity. The process pushed me to forfeit the control I so desperately wanted to impose on the situation. While the pregnant women we knew wouldn't so much as look at a deli meat sandwich for fear of the potential health risks to their unborn children, Jill and I were unable to dictate or determine what our child had been exposed to in the womb; his genetic material was, likewise, not up to us. To become adoptive parents is not to ignore the reality of the situation but to accept it.

As Shiv's grown, we have also had to accept the complicated feelings that can come along with adoption. We've never hidden the fact of his adoption from him; he knows the story of our meeting his birth mother, Mama D, just a few weeks before he was born, how we stood with her in the hospital room when he came into the world. We included pictures of her in his baby book on purpose. Sometimes he will express sadness about not knowing her or say, "I wish Mama D lived with us." In those moments, I have to fight against my instinct to smooth out the narrative, to attempt to uncomplicate his complicated feelings. To say *Everything worked out for the best!* or *But you have me and Gigi!* would be to erase the truth of what he's experiencing. He can feel sadness about his birth mother without it being a judgment against us. If he experiences grief, it is not an indication that anything is bad or wrong—on the contrary, it's healthy and normal. Still, I have to work, to bite my own tongue, in order to hold these two seemingly contradictory positions at the same time.

The impulse to sanitize the world for our children shows up in all kinds of places; we call pig meat pork and cow meat beef, allowing some kids to go years before they realize that they've been eating the very animals they find cute. We Disney-fy the world, repackaging the story of horrific historical events into media we find more palatable: *Let's memorize the rhyme-y names of Columbus's ships instead of discussing how he perpetuated the cold-blooded slaughter of natives! Let's go see a movie that depicts how much black caregivers loved and cared for the white children of their employers, even though those employers made them use an outdoor toilet!* We domesticize radical things, radical people: Jesus, Martin Luther King Jr. We smooth rough edges.

This obsessive need to smooth over speaks more to our privilege than anything else; we conflate "protection" with "good parenting," ignoring the fact that so many other parents don't have a choice when it comes to shielding their children from life's most frightening and difficult realities. My status as mother of a black son has pushed me, perhaps more than anything else, to think carefully about how I expose my child to unpleasant things and when and why I shield him from them, if at all. Though my family undoubtedly has economic privilege, and my wife benefits from white privilege, Jill and I are both painfully aware that our privilege will do nothing to protect Shiv if he is caught in a particular set of circumstances as a black male. Having a white parent and coming from a middle-class family doesn't change the fact that he is a black boy in America. The "constant worry" that many parents claim they feel when sending their kids to school, or outside to play on their own, has an added layer of reality for parents of black boys. The terror of what could someday happen to him, no matter what we might try to do to protect him, is a current running through my blood almost all the time, a recurring nightmare that wakes me, breathless. This fear is always present, though I rarely let it rise to the surface. Were I to keep it there, the fear would incapacitate me; it would render me useless as a parent. I have had to work to manage my own fear, to accept the fact that I cannot control what happens to my child. No matter what I do, I cannot guarantee his safety. In a free and open society, we cannot eliminate all risk.

A few months ago, I read an article in my local paper about kids as young as fourteen and fifteen being instructed by their parents in how to run the household, in case the parents were deported by ICE. Minutes after reading that article, I saw a post in my Facebook feed from a woman who had been to the art museum to see a collection of sculptures by Ron Mueck. Mueck's work is hyper-real, sculptures so exquisitely detailed that they could easily be mistaken for actual human bodies, though most of them are scaled up or down in size. When this Facebook friend was asked in the comments if she'd taken her children with her (they were, at the time, between seven and eleven years old), she responded that she hadn't, not wanting to expose them to the "heavy" material. The juxtaposition of these two examples of parenting was striking; what's more, having since taken my own four-year-old to that same exhibit, I find myself perplexed as to what was "heavy" about it. Even if it had been heavy, I know that Shiv will be exposed to heavy in his life, far sooner than Jill and I would like. I cannot keep the heavy from happening, but I want him to know that he can handle it when it does.

It's almost always harder to explain fully, to tell the whole story, to ask students or children to rise to the occasion where nuance or difficulty is concerned. So often it seems that what parents object to is messiness, to exposing their children to a narrative that will blow up any notion that life is orderly and predictable, that the world operates fairly, that parents can keep their kids from being exposed to unpleasant things. Of course, parents do not say this when they object. Instead, they use the word "appropriate" as a way of communicating their disapproval. *We don't think it's appropriate for this age* or *We believe this material is inappropriate,* without being able to say exactly why. Is the material inappropriate because it reflects truths that adults would rather not deal with or think about themselves?

What I've learned in the decade since my father died is that, as a general rule, we live inside a society that is profoundly bad at being in reality. Not the artificially constructed "reality" of television shows that bear that label, but the truth of what we are: humans who often treat our fellow human beings cruelly, who are capable of great evil as well as great good; mortal creatures, animals that will, someday, each one of us, necessarily die. What's more, what's worse—we have no sense of what it costs to be in such denial. I've had colleagues and friends—grown adults—literally cover their ears with their hands rather than hear me talk about the importance of making a will, of discussing final wishes, of plotting financials to make the inevitable even just a little bit easier. There is a numbness, an estrangement, that keeps us from relating, from telling the truth, from equipping our children for what is inevitably coming. We are so disembodied, so disconnected from the processes of the body and the inevitability of the body's failure and the materiality of bodies—sinew, muscle, bone, blood.

In his book *Cooked,* Michael Pollan defines disgust as the human response to anything that reminds us that we're animals. As a feeling, disgust has a biological function—it keeps us from eating things that might kill us, like rotten meat. But I can't help wondering if it hasn't also sterilized us to the point that we've completely forgotten that we are, as it turns out, animals. As one of my son's main ambassadors to this planet, I feel responsible for reporting the truth, as best I know it.

And so Jill and I choose to parent our son in ways that often alarm other parents. He cuts vegetables with a real knife; he stands, as he has since he was much younger, at a hot stove and helps us cook. Though he's not yet cut himself, he has been splattered by hot grease, felt the sensation on his skin; he has a healthy respect for what cooking oil can do. At the playground, he has fallen. Rather than follow him around, I establish myself on a bench, making sure that Shiv knows where to find me if he needs me, and then I take out a book or my journal. My ears sometimes perk up at the sound of a disagreement between him and another child, but I keep my butt glued to the bench unless Shiv calls for me; even then, I try to encourage him to find a way to work the problem out on his own. While I often strategize with him in the car before and after, debriefing whatever just went down, only once have I directly interfered in playground drama.

Still, other parents seem to feel the need to jump in, sometimes even running over to "assist" Shiv as he climbs, though he has not asked for and doesn't need help. We have had friends and acquaintances express alarm at the tools we keep in the backyard—hanging on a hook but still accessible—shears, a rake, a hoe. Even when he was a crawling toddler, parents of kids his age would move things off of shelves in our house when they came to visit, the background implication being that, were we more responsible parents, we would have done so ourselves.

We strive to live in reality, to raise Shiv inside of reality and not magical thinking. Last night, he asked about Tillie, the beloved old dog of his auntie Coco and uncle John; we explained that they had made the decision to end Tillie's life, as she was no longer able to move on her own.

"They asked their doctor to come and give her medicine that will end her life." (By default, I almost said "put her to sleep" but refused. Adults may know what that euphemism means, but I didn't want to confuse or mislead him.)

"The doctor going to kill her?"

"Yes, sweetie. It will happen quickly and then Tillie won't be hurting anymore."

He contemplated this. Jill, who grew up with dogs and has said goodbye to many animals in her time, explained that we had done the same with Dolly, the terrier we had when Shiv was first born.

"Did you hold her and tell her [his voice dropping to a stage whisper], 'Goodbye, Dolly, I love you'?"

"Yes, sweetie. It was very hard, but we knew that it was the right thing to do."

Then—a choice. There was a natural opening to tell him the story of his grandfather's death, how his grandmother and I placed an order to take my father off a respirator when it became clear that he would not be waking up, that his lungs would never again work on their own. How it was the hardest thing I've ever done. How loving someone can be hard work, can mean forfeiting what feels good to us in favor of what's best for them, sort of like his birth mother did when she placed him with us almost five years ago.

After I told him the story, he responded, "I miss Nanaji," he said, employing the Hindi word for "mother's father."

"I miss him, too, dude."

"You get sad when you think about him. It makes you cry."

"Yeah, it does."

"It's okay to cry, Mama. Sometimes I get sad about my birth mother and I cry, too."

Powerful though the urge is, I know that to shelter my child would only render him dependent on me; my task is to prepare him, not protect him. On the ten-year anniversary of my father's death, I had two tattoos inked onto my wrists: on the right, a stylized rendering of the initials that Shiv shares with my dad, SCM; on the left, a line drawing of a lotus, a potent symbol within both Hinduism and Buddhism. Thich Nhat Hanh, the Zen Buddhist monk, is famous for his saying "No mud, no lotus." Without suffering, there is no growth. I work to keep myself grounded in reality, so that I can raise a child who will thrive inside of it.

Raising Shiv

We never had to tell our son that he was black. It was not a thing we had to name for him but something he gathered on his own. He was quite young, probably two, when he presented this fact to us for confirmation: "I black?"

This did not surprise me; I don't remember a time in my own life when I didn't know that I was brown. I am gravely aware of what language can do, what it can generate, what it can erase. Labels are not neutral, least of all the ones tied to identity. Giving Shiv descriptors to apply to himself—brave, kind, boy, black—formalizes his identity and provides him with different ways to define himself, like those crystals we grew in elementary science class, strings suspended in sugar water, accumulating more layers with each passing day.

As anyone who has spent even a little bit of time with a two-year-old knows, a toddler's first linguistic obsession is identification. They hold up something: "What dis?" You tell them. Over and over and over again. Occasionally, you struggle to recall the names of objects you have taken for granted or to articulate the answer to unintentional toddler koans; what sound *does* a giraffe make?

Questions like these were prompted by Shiv's obsession with his *Visual Dictionary,* a doorstop of a book that contains an illustrated catalog of almost every concrete noun you can imagine, organized by category, from creatures to weapons to food items to sports. From the start, he was particularly taken with the animal section, as many kids that age often are. He'd spend half an hour turning pages and pointing to illustrations so that we would say the names aloud: *albatross, tern, condor, eagle.* As he grew in his knowledge, watching him was like watching a tiny Adam, tasked with naming the creatures in Eden: *dis woodpecker, thas hummin-bird, is ostrich, Mama—no can fly.* Words are declarative, words are generative, they make the conceptual real, they provide meaning. We identify something, we name it, and suddenly it exists.

Jill and I made the decision to adopt together, the end result of several years of talking and thinking through our future. When we fell in love, I was young—nineteen—but already knew that I wanted to have kids. Conversely, Jill was thirty-eight and had previously decided not to have children. Committing to each other was a bold leap of faith for both of us; we met because I was a student in one of Jill's classes at Rice University, which sounds more like the plot for a scandalous TV drama than the formula for a successful long-term relationship. But the doubts of those around us were assuaged over time. The only question that hung unsettled in our life was the one about having kids.

The idea of becoming pregnant and giving birth had always interested me, but ending up in a long-term relationship with a woman complicated that vision. My dear friend Wayne agreed to be my "someday" sperm donor when we were both in college, but as we got older and that prospect became less theoretical, it also started to feel more complicated. Plus, there was something about the whole idea that made Jill nervous or, at least, didn't inspire her excitement or enthusiasm.

Adoption did. Jill felt pulled, called by the thought that we could provide a home for a child who needed one. It was a vision I could be easily drawn into—two of my good friends were adopted as infants—and helped solve the question of genetics. Our task would be to nurture a person who was already here. Only, what kind of person would that be? Our application to adopt included a form asking us to check the boxes that corresponded to the traits we were comfortable with in an adoptive child: male, female, twins, Caucasian, Hispanic, Asian, African American, Native American. There were also boxes for the baby's alcohol and drug exposure as well as family history of mental illness.

That piece of paper tied me up in all kinds of knots. I was being given the option to choose my child, to exert some power over the process, and the consequences related to the form were real. Though I had embraced adoption wholeheartedly, there was still a part of me that wanted the same baby experience as "everybody else," but the form served as a blatant reminder that I wasn't getting it. Adoption is an industry where a great deal of money changes hands and "customer satisfaction" is a factor. I, however, was attached to the conventional narrative that adoption is inherently more noble than other ways of becoming a parent. My response to that form—namely, my hesitancy in signing up to potentially parent a black child—interrupted any sense of nobility I might have conjured for myself. Filling out a form to adopt a child felt a little too similar to filling out an order form, especially because the pricing varied, depending on the type of child. Our adoption agency had two different fee schedules: one that was standard and one that was for children considered "difficult to place."

And which children qualified as difficult to place, you might ask? Black children.

Part of me firmly believed that Jill and I would provide an excellent home for any child. We were thoughtful, we had re-sources, and we would do what we needed to do. But another part of me wondered if I was being naive. Were we prepared for all the issues that we would inevitably face if we became the parents of a black child? This was circa 2011, before Tamir, before Trayvon, before I had thought meaningfully about the fraught complexi-ties of being black in America, but I was aware enough to know that there would be challenges. Were we the right people to raise a black child? Could we do right by that child? Would our child someday wake up and think, *What the hell am I doing with you people?* Was that a responsibility we were willing to take on?

These questions made me uncomfortable because they forced me to reckon with my own latent racism. It meant admitting the extent to which I had become self-congratulatory about my own social consciousness. I would no longer be able to ignore or po-litely shake my head at things that I'd spent my life ignoring or politely shaking my head at: history, literature, art, news, politics, and current events that weren't "about me" or "mine." I'm certain it's possible to become the parent of a black child and continue to ignore those things (though not without some measured effort), but I knew that I wouldn't be able to. It's one thing to know that institutional racism exists or to grapple with it intellectually. But to be confronted by its existence on a regular basis is, as I would soon learn, a game changer.

The adoption form gave me an out. I could have said, *You know what? I'm not up for this.* And that's exactly why it made me so uncomfortable, mirroring back a version of myself that I didn't particularly like or want to look at. When it came down to filling out the form, though, neither Jill nor I could bear the thought of leaving even a single box unchecked. If a birth mother looked at us and decided we weren't the right family for her child, okay. But what child could we possibly, preemptively, say no to? With Jill looking over my shoulder, I checked every box.

Nearly nine months to the day after submitting our paperwork, Jill and I were matched with our son's birth mother; she, like our son's birth father, is black. From that moment, Jill and I were clear about what we *wouldn't* do—perpetuate notions of color blindness or further narratives about a "post-racial" society and raise a black child as if he wasn't. Even as the term "post-racial" was being called out as fantasy, it felt more like an absurdity in the daily context of raising Shiv. It infuriated me to hear people declare, "I don't see color," as if it were some kind of virtuous position; to treat my child as if his color is irrelevant is to erase him and to deny the fact that his color is all that some people will see about him.

Knowing what we didn't want to do still left us with little sense of what we *would* do. Models for race-conscious parenting, though more prevalent than they've ever been, are still few and far between. We couldn't speak to Shiv about being black, but Jill and I have had our own varied experiences with prejudice as gay women. Growing up with two moms also meant that there would be added elements of identity and prejudice for Shiv to tackle.

For a while, we held our worries, concerns, and plans in an orbit around Shiv, not directly involving him or discussing them with him. At the start, our parenting concerns were fairly universal anyway: sleeping and eating schedules, daily logistics, managing behavior, doctor's appointments, and so on. We were already used to living as an interracial, same-sex couple before adding Shiv to the mix; long looks from strangers were not new to us. As a brown woman in America, I have also grown accustomed to unsolicited comments from strangers about my skin color and questions about my ethnic background. (Just before I wrote this sentence, a waitress told me that I "didn't look Indian," something I've heard my entire life.)

But adopting Shiv dramatically increased the amount of attention that even I was accustomed to receiving. Part of this is due to Shiv—he is a wildly charismatic human, thoroughly extroverted, always seeking to connect with those around him. And the other part is that our family doesn't look like most other families; we don't make sense to people when they look at us, at least not at first. When Shiv was still too young to understand, I felt a sense of fraught anticipation. At some point, the difference that he and our family represented to the broader world would begin to register with him. And, at some point, perhaps the same point, our family would begin to receive attention that was not well intended. When you're living as a person of color in America, it's a question not of *if* but of *when*. For each month that passed without incident, I carried the knowledge that it wouldn't last.

As a southerner, I find it telling that my son's first experience of blatant prejudice took place in Portland, Oregon, supposed bastion of tolerance and progressivism. Shiv, my mom, and I were spending a few days in the city before traveling down to Eugene, where my best friend was about to graduate with her doctorate from the University of Oregon. One beautifully sunny day, we took public transportation to the Portland zoo, where Shiv correctly identified a bald eagle without any hints from me (thanks, *Visual Dictionary*) and delighted in the sight of his first live polar bear. After a fair amount of trekking, he discovered a shaded play area that included a giant sandpit filled with digger trucks, shovels, and buckets; there were at least ten other kids hard at work when we arrived. My mom went off to find some food while I sat on a nearby bench, watching out of the corner of one eye the way parents do.

Shiv was one month away from turning three, and I was trying to let him work out social conflicts on his own; he had a year of preschool under his belt, where they encouraged kids to do the same, so I left him alone until I heard what was unmistakably his cry of distress. I found him in a standoff with an older white boy, whom I later discovered was five years old, over the possession of a particular dump truck. "Black boys can't play here," the boy told me. I froze.

I do not think Shiv completely grasped *why* what was said was hurtful, but he understood the intention behind the words. In my brain, I scrambled to uncover some thoughtful piece of parenting advice I might have filed away for just such a situation. I don't know exactly what I said to the other kid, though I remember saying something. I wanted to scold him, but I also knew that he was parroting back something he'd heard a grown-up say, with full awareness that it was an insult, though not perhaps of its full significance.

After a conversation with the boy's babysitter (who was also white and completely mortified), and a conversation between the babysitter and boy, he and Shiv reconciled and wound up playing together peacefully in the sand. At this point in his life, Shiv was still learning about unkindness in general, attempting to grasp why people might be hurtful to others in a whole host of contexts, from villains in fairy tales to mean kids on the playground; he had not yet distinguished that some people would be motivated to treat him differently because of the color of his skin.

It didn't take long. Less than two years later, Jill, Shiv, and I were enjoying another beautiful afternoon, this time at the Houston Livestock Show and Rodeo, an enormous affair that features an impressive carnival midway and vendors selling every type of fried food you can imagine. That was the first year that Shiv was tall enough to graduate from the kiddie rides and gain access to an additional crop of rides and fun houses. As he stood in line to gain entrance to an underwater-themed fun house, it became clear to me that the ticket taker was ignoring him. There had been some jostling, and the line wasn't necessarily well formed, so he waited patiently on the stairs for her to call him forward. He was the only child of color in line; the ticket taker was white.

At this point, I felt myself begin to fume—even writing about it, my hands get shaky—and though I knew what I was seeing, I checked in with Jill. "Am I being paranoid, or . . . ?" She knew immediately what I meant, which was a relief. We were both still hesitant to intervene, knowing that doing so might only make the situation worse, but also devastated by the look of disappointment and confusion on Shiv's face. Gathering him up to leave and get in line for another ride would feel like a punishment to him. Then the ticket taker actually scolded Shiv, implying that he had cut in the line, sending him back a few places, which made our decision for us. Jill, the white mom, intervened, much to the woman's surprise. She softened, though not enough to smile at him or tell him to "have fun!" as she had with the other kids, when letting him in. Jill and I, both working to wrangle our anger, met Shiv at the exit, where he proceeded to tell us how cool it had been inside. Suddenly, his face fell. "Why that lady was mean to me and not the other kids?"

We sighed, took a deep breath, told him the truth. *Some white people are ugly to black people. Some white people think that they're better than people who aren't white. It's really unfair and we're sorry. You didn't do anything wrong.*

———

Growing up in the 1980s, I was sold a cultural narrative of *all colors of the rainbow are beautiful, but we don't talk about racism!* As a brown, queer woman, I can testify that sentiment didn't work for me, and I was unwilling to sell Shiv a story that I knew was more wishful thinking than truth. We couch color-blind rhetoric as hopeful, even well intentioned, but that ignores the day-to-day reality of people of color and undermines our experience with feel-good rhetoric. Providing Shiv with a censored view of the way our society works might feel easier in the short term, but that willful ignorance would leave him completely unprepared to face the world as it is.

But telling a small child the truth about the ugliness in the world is a very unpleasant task, and we Americans tend to opt for a lot of erasing instead. The positive, upward trajectory of *Progress!* that's taught in every American history class means denying the racism and violence that has occurred, and continues to occur, in this country. We like to focus more on all of the things that are "better now," while refusing to talk about what still needs work. Whether I wanted to or not, I knew that I could not rewrite history or shield Shiv from uncovering unpleasant realities on his own; how would he feel when he discovered I'd kept the truth from him all along?

The most potent resource I would encounter to help me develop a parenting approach in response to this question came, oddly enough, from an episode of *This American Life* that I happened to listen to on a morning walk. Episode 557, "Birds & Bees," examines three topics generally considered dangerous territory to discuss with kids: sex, race, and death. The episode describes its middle segment as tackling "the other facts of life that you don't want to have to explain to children because you wish they were not facts or a part of life at all." Narrated by the comedian W. Kamau Bell, the segment describes his personal struggle to determine just what to say to his two young mixed-race daughters about race in

America. He describes two metaphoric pools: the race pool and the racism pool. The race pool, he recounts, is filled with positive stories of black achievement, heartwarming books, and diverse TV shows. Introducing his daughters to this pool was no problem and a no-brainer. But the racism pool—where the rest of the stories live and which is a lot less fun to swim in—Bell avoided and then felt guilty for avoiding.

After a particularly infuriating experience with racism in his own neighborhood, Bell organizes a public meeting to discuss the issues. At the forum, he meets a young black woman, Kadijah Means, a high school senior and Bay Area activist, who so impresses him with her understanding of "the broad strokes and the nuances" of race and racism that he decides to interview her father, in order to learn how to raise such a well-informed and self-assured daughter.

What Bell learns surprises him: Kadijah's father, Cliff Means, had not only taken his daughter to swim in the racism pool at an early age; he had thrown her in the deep end. By age five, she had learned about slavery, Jim Crow, and historically racist policing policies in their home state of California. Cliff Means did not hold anything back, nor did he soften the edges of the rough truths he was asking his young daughter to swallow.

It is unfashionable in a helicopter parenting culture to push young children to swallow difficult, or even unpleasant, truths. With the impulse to protect comes, necessarily, an implication that children are unable to handle complexity and disappointment. To deliberately ask your child to see the ugly truth about racism in our country's past and present can feel, on first blush, extreme and unnecessary, cruel and perverse. Why introduce things that will interrupt his innocence? Won't the world do that eventually anyway?

And that's the point. As I took a long walk and listened to Kadijah and Cliff Means's story, I realized what Means did for his daughter—he armed her with knowledge. No one could surprise her or catch her off guard or insult her because she already knew the whole story herself. She knew how to see racism, and she also knew how to separate it from herself. This was the gift her father gave her. He knew that keeping the truth from her was not a form of protection; rather, it made her more vulnerable.

I find that most, if not all, of the parents I speak to (who are mostly, if not all, white) are alarmed by the "deep end of the swimming pool" approach to talking to kids about race; it feels extreme, unpleasant, unnecessary. Many remain convinced that race "just isn't going to be an issue" for our kids the way it has been for kids in the past. Some of them even seem to believe that by talking to their children about race, they will somehow make race and discrimination real for their children in a way that wouldn't happen otherwise.

The research begs to differ. Mahzarin Banaji, a Harvard University scientist who is best known for co-developing the famous Implicit Association Test, says that children as young as age three can pick up and parrot racist behavior within a few days of being exposed to it. A study conducted by University of Massachusetts–Amherst researcher Lisa Scott found that by nine months, infants have an easier time reading the emotional expressions of adults within groups they interact the most with; no wonder, then, that babies will display a preference for the faces of those who share their skin color. By the time they are preschoolers, our kids have already begun to differentiate how they play with children of their same race from how they play with "others."

I think about white students I've taught, who come from liberal, progressive families but have been raised not to speak of race at all. Even as high school students, they struggle to understand the distinction between identifying race-related realities and saying something racist. They are such beginners, and I can't help wondering to what extent that is due to the discomfort of the adults in their lives, who sold their kids an easy story rather than deal with the messy complexity of the truth.

In 2016, when my school's holiday calendar aligned with the opening of the National Museum of African American History and Culture, I decided that I would take Shiv. Like all Smithsonian institutions, the NMAAHC is vast, with multiple floors and wings that would take days to explore fully. I was there with a four-year-old, so I knew I had about two hours, max, before his attention gave out and his restlessness kicked in. With that in mind, we stepped onto a long escalator, then into a large elevator which took us several stories underground, the glass sides of the cab revealing dates written on the wall, flashing us back in time until we stepped out into the fifteenth century, the start of the African slave trade. This was what I had come to show him; it was why we were there.

The trip was my attempt to control his exposure to ideas about race, to get ahead of the game when it came to difficult topics I knew he would inevitably encounter, no matter how much I might try to shield him. I control the food he eats, when he sleeps, the media he consumes—why would I leave the first time he learned about slavery to chance? How much he would absorb I did not know, but I felt I owed him the truth.

What the visit will mean to him, what he will remember, I cannot say. He was uncharacteristically quiet as we walked through the exhibits and quickly asked me to pick him up and carry him—"Hold you, Mama"—though I knew he was not physically tired.

At sixty-five pounds, he was not easy to heft, but nothing about that visit was supposed to be easy.

He was far from the only child his age there, though it was only black children I saw and mostly black adults, with a visible minority of white faces. Their presence made me wonder whom the museum was for, who the assumed audience might be. I was clearly not the only one who had thought to bring their black child. I was surprised by how quickly Shiv picked up on the feel of the space, how somber and withdrawn he became. He pointed to specific parts of the exhibit to ask questions: a pair of child-sized shackles struck him the most; he was unable to understand why anyone would want to treat a child that way.

In our family we believe that evil is not inherent but chosen or taught. Therefore, we speak not of *bad people* and *good people* but of *bad ideas, bad choices*. There is danger, I feel, in fooling ourselves into thinking that all the people who perpetuated a slaveholding state were somehow evil, different from us, separate, removed. A comforting thought. One I have learned to refuse.

An artistic rendering of a slave auction was the last thing Shiv asked me to explain. "Mama, I don't want to talk about this stuff anymore." We moved quickly through the Civil War, into Reconstruction, into the segregated Pullman car of the Jim Crow era, and upward (literally—even the NMAAHC is not immune to that classic Western conception of time) into the present day. I have a photograph of Shiv standing, smiling, in front of a collection of four quotes that serve as the final panel inside the history galleries: one, a statement from the Chicago Commission on Race Relationships; another, a quote from Barack Obama; the third, Alicia Garza's declaration "Our lives matter"; and finally, Maya Angelou's affirmation "I am the dream and the hope of the slave."

Since that time at the Portland zoo, Shiv's encounters around race have been fairly innocuous and mostly coded; I see them more than he does. I grew up spending a great deal of time as the only non-white person in white spaces, and those uncomfortable, alienating experiences are less likely to occur in Houston than in Memphis. In both his hometown and mine, Shiv and I will sometimes find ourselves the only non-white people in the room at birthday parties, on playgrounds. It is a space that feels comfortable, or at least familiar to me. But Shiv's presence adds an extra layer to the experience, one that makes me itchy and in a hurry to get it over with, moved by my instinctive desire to protect my child.

Last summer, at a pool party in a white part of town, Shiv was one of only two black people among at least a hundred. I stayed close by because he was still learning how to swim but tried hard not to interfere. He wound up near a group of white boys who looked about six or seven; because Shiv is so big for his age, he is often drawn to kids his size who end up being much older than him and whom he tries to imitate.

Instinctively, I knew the boys were making fun of him even though I could not hear their words: their body language and laughter were enough. I moved closer and saw Shiv point to me. "*That's* your mom?" the older boys asked skeptically. He nodded. They kept asking him questions, which he either didn't understand or chose to ignore. "Can you talk?" the boys asked. They started to speak louder, to overenunciate their words as if he were deaf or stupid. Were these boys just being jerks, or was it extra because my kid is black? How much did race play into the dynamic? Not *if* but *how much*. Even if kids can't articulate, they still understand and see difference. They internalize what is external in their world. I was eager for the moment I could pull Shiv from the pool to go inside and eat cake.

Even in our own neighborhood, which is wonderfully diverse and blessedly safe, where kids ride their bikes out in the street and parents and caregivers keep a collective eye on them, Shiv was recently told to "go back home to his white parents" by the visiting aunt of a couple of neighborhood kids he's played with in the past. I had had a conversation a few months before with one of those same playmates in which I'd had to work fairly hard to convince her that my son did, in fact, have two moms and did not, in fact, have a daddy. Genuinely perplexed, she kept staring up at me as if there *had* to be some mistake. Now, if she happens to stop by when Jill's not at home, she will ask, "Where's his other mama?" We often serve as others' learning curve, on one level or another.

It's difficult, perhaps impossible, to separate the layers of our family's dynamics: the attention we attract as same-sex parents; the attention we attract as a mixed-race family; the attention we attract simply through our respective personalities. So while it may not be a productive exercise, I often wonder if what feels so essential to me now would still be on our radar if we did not have a black son.

I am always surprised when others are surprised to hear that Shiv pays attention to skin color and that he has from a young age. For him, it does not yet have the baggage that it has for us; often his observations are a simple celebration of representation and sameness. Of the little girl he played with at Memphis International Airport: "She black, like me!" Of the little black boy with a shaved head flying a kite in Wynton Marsalis's book *Squeak, Rumble,*

Whomp! Whomp! Whomp!—"Thas me! I in the book!" When our friends express surprise at this awareness, I am reminded that the extent to which this is *not* a part of their consciousness is the same as their unawareness of how ingrained it is into mine.

At another birthday party, a woman on the playground pointed to my son and his buddy rocking on one of those spring-mounted plastic creatures and said, "So those are your boys?"

"No," I responded, "just the one on the right—that's my son."

"Oh," she said, clearly flummoxed. "Oh—I saw you talking to them both and I just assumed . . ." She trailed off. Both my son and his friend are black and were the only two black boys on the playground. They are the same age, but they don't look at all alike. To her in that moment perhaps, they did.

So much of what we encounter on a daily basis are these kinds of moments, moments that everyone wants to tell me are likely innocuous, moments that I myself tend to disclaim as "little things." Perhaps these assumptions and questions individually don't feel like much, but they build up, even over a short lifetime of my son's four and a half years. What has been most revealing about this is tracking Jill's reaction; as a woman who has benefited from white privilege her whole life, being on the receiving end of these racially charged moments is new for her. She's witnessed and observed them her whole life, but watching them circle around your child is another thing. How many times have we been met with a comment about football whenever someone notices how big Shiv is for his age? How often have we witnessed an adult stranger treat our child just differently enough to have us suspect that it might be related to his color? I don't want these moments to rule us or determine our behavior in the world, but to have them ignored or discounted repeatedly is disheartening and exhausting.

We were recently gifted a beautiful book about the life of Josephine Baker, vividly written with distinctive illustrations. At first Shiv looked through the book himself, flipping pages and focusing on the pictures—he is a dancer, after all, so he did not need words for those images to translate—then that night, he requested that I read it to him at bedtime. For a picture book it's fairly long, and I thought that he might lose interest partway through, but he insisted that we read the whole thing. I learned much that I didn't know about Baker, who was tremendously inventive and brave, but the section that drew Shiv's attention most had to do not with her dancing but with the race riots in East St. Louis.

"Why the white people want to hurt the black people?" he asked. It's a question to which I always want to respond, *I don't know, baby,* as if there's no explanation for such hatred, though of course there is. But how do I explain thousands of years of white supremacy to a four-year-old? How do I explain how it undergirds essentially everything around him, from this book about Josephine Baker to the very circumstances that created our family?

Then I reminded myself, *This is not the first nor will it be by any means the last conversation we have about race,* so I focused on the question at hand and responded to it as simply and honestly as I could. "There are some white people who believe that they are better than black people simply because of the color of their skin. These white people were, and still are, threatened when black people try to assert themselves or create better lives for themselves. And sometimes when people feel threatened, they become violent."

"But Gigi is white!" he said with alarm, as if just realizing this for the first time. Connecting the abstract white people represented on the page with the real-life white person he lives with and loves.

This complexity and its attendant baggage are a lot for anyone to hold, let alone a four-year-old. But he will have to hold it, all his life, an inheritance that will constantly shape-shift; just when he thinks he's wrangled it, it will alter in his hands.

For most of my life, I have been afraid of anger: my own and other people's. This is true to such an extent that it feels disingenuous to write the phrase "my own anger," as it is a feeling I have trained myself to deny or push away or disassociate from for so long. As a girl, I sensed that anger was unbecoming; as a brown girl in a white world, I felt anger was a trait destined to relegate me to the realm of easily dismissible, further proof of the stereotype.

Sara Ahmed, self-described "feminist killjoy," writes about our culture's relentless obsession with positivity and the detriment that brings. To kill joy, she says, can be "to open a life, to make room for life, to make room for possibility, for chance." Certain ways of being are not even visible under the glaring light of our stubborn bright-sidedness. By focusing on the light, we conveniently forget and devalue the territory in the shadows.

I grew up with a lot of privilege and, like many woman, was raised to be pleasant. But becoming Shiv's parent has created, or maybe revealed, a deep well of anger in me. It makes sense to be angry. Anger is, at times, the only logical response, the necessary first step. I am late to this party, but I have learned that anger, properly processed, becomes fuel. Resisting anger for so long only led me to fear, and I refuse to put my child in the same position.

I owe him honesty. I owe him the truth. I owe him a willingness to sit in ambiguity with him, to refuse to tell the convenient story or to pretend that I myself have arrived at some full understanding. "And still you are called to struggle," writes Ta-Nehisi Coates in his letter to his son, Samori, "not because it assures you victory but because it assures you an honorable and sane life."

Making Space

I never thought I would be a dance mom, but here I am, kneeling on the linoleum entrance of a high school auditorium on dress rehearsal day, fishing a black makeup pencil out of a Ziploc bag to touch up my son's eyeliner. "It tickles, Mama," he says, standing in his black leggings and ballet shoes, his three-and-a-half-year-old belly visible under the cream fabric of his "sailor shirt" costume. After double-checking his dinosaur backpack for the recommended supplies (snacks, extra makeup, quiet toys), I zip it up and help him pull it onto his shoulders.

As we move into the line that had formed behind the "dancer drop-off" table, I take a moment to absorb the pre-recital chaos: sequins, glitter, hair spray, bright lipstick, tights, dry-cleaning bags full of costumes. And girls. Every single one of the other dancers is female. Shiv is already the only boy in his five-person dance class—a fact that he had never once commented on—but here he is about to be the only boy backstage (minus the parent volunteers who are dads—I do see a few). I kneel down next to him, feeling obliged to prep him:

"Hey, buddy, you know how there are lots of other kids here? And they're mostly girls?"

"Uh-huh."

"Well, I just think it's really awesome that you're here, because you love to dance and that's what you have in common with all of these girls. And it doesn't matter that you're the only boy, in fact I think it makes you really brave. And I'm proud of you for doing what you enjoy."

"Mom, I *know*," he says, shifting his weight beneath his back-pack, sounding exactly like a teenager demonstrating that it was I who'd needed that little pep talk, not him.

We reach the head of the line. I give my cell phone number to a parent volunteer, who issues me a sticker that will allow me to pick him up after the rehearsal; another volunteer, whose Forever 21–style wardrobe I try and fail not to judge, stands smiling and ready to escort Shiv backstage.

"What's his name?" she asks. I prompt him to answer, as I always do, even though by now we both have a sense of how it's going to play out. It's kind of a thing, when Shiv is asked for his name. He says it clearly, and other kids can parrot it back just fine, but adults, who are anticipating a name they recognize, or who do not expect his name to go with a boy who looks like him, almost always puzzle over it, as the woman standing in front of us proceeds to do.

"Shay?" She cocks her head at him.

He says his name again, more firmly this time: "No, *Shiv*."

"Jeff?" Now she's looking up at me with puzzlement.

Shiv also looks to me for backup, so I jump in. "Shiv, like Shiva," I explain. "Rhymes with 'give.' S-h-i-v, Shiv."

The woman smiles warmly at both of us and takes my son's

hand. "Okay then, Mr. Shiv, are you ready to dance?" He grins at her, barely offering me a wave goodbye as I tell him I'll be back to pick him up later.

We knew it wouldn't be simple, giving Shiv his name. Nothing about parenting Shiv is simple, because we're this at once recognizable yet totally unfamiliar amalgam of a twenty-first-century family: white mom, brown mom, black son. We push a lot of cultural buttons; our friends joke that our holiday cards could double as ads for United Colors of Benetton. We draw attention without trying to, and the world doesn't always know what to do with us. We are still a novelty for most of the people we encounter, and almost everywhere we go, one of us or all of us are in the minority. This has become normal, but even in our own home, where parenting is not public, it can feel fraught. There is a consciousness about our family's visibility, what it means, how our choices will be judged, and, on top of that, the extra consciousness of trying not to let that factor into our decisions too much.

Our son is a sweet boy, well behaved, if willful, and most of the time he is exhausting and fun, like every other three-year-old I know. But because of who he is, who his parents are, and the various spaces he occupies, we spend a lot of time crashing like bumper cars into people's assumptions, questions, and disbelief. Even when doing something as simple as telling people his name.

"Is that Indian or something?" they ask. (Most don't know the exact reference, but his name almost always rings a bell.)

My son's name is, in fact, "Indian or something," and as it turns out, it suits him perfectly. When our adoption agency matched us with his birth mother, she was thirty-six weeks pregnant and thought she was carrying a girl. A second ultrasound, at which we were breathlessly in attendance, seemed to confirm the gender. For seventeen days, the "It's a Girl!" ultrasound printout hung suspended on the front of the fridge with a Gustav Klimt magnet. The ultrasound was why we didn't have a name picked out for our son when he was born. We weren't even sure we could call him our son when we left the hospital that first night, unable to stay past visiting hours; the nurse on duty was fairly hostile to Jill and me and refused to issue us wristbands that would allow us to remain overnight, even though our adoption agency had assured us we would be entitled to them. As with many things, in retrospect I think we ought to have pushed, asked to speak to a supervisor, but in that space of dazzling vulnerability and uncertainty about what was coming next, we were scared to challenge anything. So instead we drove home.

We wanted our son to share his initials with my dad, Subhash, who died in 2006. I briefly considered naming Shiv after my dad outright, but it seemed like a lot for a baby to carry, the name of a dead man, not to mention a name that isn't easy for most people to spell or pronounce. We knew that we would be giving our child—regardless of gender—Jill's last name, Carroll, for a middle name, and that the baby and I would share my last name, Mehra. To figure out the missing piece, Jill Googled "Indian baby boy names S" and I called my mom. We moved down the list unsuccessfully for a few minutes, before they both asked, within seconds of each other, Jill to my face and Mom through my ear, "What about Shiv?"

Shiva is one of the three primary deities in Hinduism, a warrior and a dancer, a yogi and conqueror of the ego, a god of contradictions, a container for things that do not, at first glance, seem to fit together. *Shiv Carroll Mehra*—the more we get to know him, the more we believe we got the name just right.

Of course, "shiv" has another connotation. When you look up "shiv" in *Urban Dictionary* it means something very different: a prison knife, or the act of stabbing someone with one. The helpful example sentence given is *Ima shiv you, bitch!*

We knew this when we picked the name, yet we named our son Shiv anyway. Naively, perhaps, but I saw the decision as a firm assertion of what kind of world we would raise our child to be a part of, what context he would occupy. It was always going to be challenging for him—two moms and three colors in one family—so I didn't see the point in bowing to the hypothetical misinterpretation of others. Better to arm him with ancient Sanskrit and a badass namesake and then raise a kid who could carry the weight of both.

Being a nontraditional family means constantly navigating and questioning public perceptions and stereotypes while also being occupied with the same mundane tasks and activities as every other family: bedtime stories, pancakes on Saturday morning, trips to the neighborhood pool. This can create a kind of cultural whiplash. Some people think our family is adorable, the very embodiment of twenty-first-century America, a testament to the power of love and an ever-expanding definition of family; some people think our family is an abomination, everything wrong with America today, evidence of a civilization in decline. The latter comes with a certain freedom, the ability to create our own traditions and expectations, precisely because we are challenging long-held conventions. Jill and I joke that the biggest perk of being a lesbian— aside from the free and guaranteed birth control—was the fact that we largely got to opt out of the cultural gender norms that seem to descend upon our straight friends, particularly when they get married and/or have kids. We thought that we were aligned with our friends in principle, but then suddenly they're planning a wedding or raising their children and these deeply gendered, traditional assertions come out of their mouths, like some kind of pre-programming we didn't know was there. Of course Jill and I have a bit of an advantage, being gay. Much as (some parts of) society wishes to normalize us now, Jill and I have a history of being outsiders, both as individuals and as a couple. Coming out is itself a move outside of the familiar, and it's a move that necessitates— or creates—at least a modicum of courage when it comes to disregarding what others think. When the norms don't apply to you, you have to make up another way to live, which can be difficult, isolating work. But it's also freeing: it *proves* that, in fact, another way is possible. It reveals how much we are choosing, even (or especially) when we act as if we have no choice.

A few months ago, I saw a post on Instagram from a woman I don't know well. She has a son, who at the time was about fourteen months old, and is pregnant with her second child. She'd posted side-by-side photos of her son, before and after getting a haircut:

> *This baby's hair reached the bottom of his nose in the front, and it's longer in the back. Everyone called him a girl, and he walked with his head leaned back so he could see. Since he's not a girl, we can't pull back the front into a clip or a bow. So . . . we broke down and got his hair cut.*

As an English teacher, I spend a fair amount of time working to convince my students that words matter—where we use them, how we use them, which ones we use.

> We can't pull back the front into a clip or a bow.
>
> We *won't* pull back the front into a clip or a bow.
>
> We *don't want to* pull back the front into a clip or a bow.

I think about how we were initially told that Shiv would be a girl. It's a story that we recount with humor: *He was being shy!* or *I guess the tech just wasn't paying close attention!* This, too, is a symptom of a culture that is uncomfortable with vagary or uncertainty, the idea that even a fetus in the womb might be misidentified, assigned the wrong sex or gender. We are so invested in the correctness of these designations, so troubled by the muddling of the waters.

When you adopt, the baby's sex is already determined by the time you match with a birth mother. Jill and I had not specified boy or girl when we registered with our agency, but for some reason I imagined us with a boy. Whenever I pictured us with a child, or had a dream with a baby in it, that baby was always male. When we heard, "It's a girl!" I thought about whether my expectations or plans should change. We enlisted our friend Kym for hair help; black hair was not something either one of us had experience with, and we knew that it was an important matter. I planned to buy posters of Venus and Serena Williams for her room, because I wanted there to be strong black women for her to look at every day. We asked for gender-neutral clothes and bedding; we painted the nursery green as a way of resisting that whole pink situation. Both Jill and I had been girls who chafed under the aesthetic expectations placed on our gender, and while we knew we wouldn't be able to give our daughter a *blank* canvas, we wanted to give her a wide palette.

Then Shiv was born, and when I saw the doctor raise that taut red body into the air, the fact of his being a boy was subsumed into the larger miracle of his sudden emergence. In that moment, we were gobsmacked so completely by the fact that our child was finally here, an actual person, a baby we could hold, that we did not give much thought to what it would or should mean that we now had a son.

Right away, we had to decide what conventions we would hold on to and which we would challenge or ignore. Did it matter if our son wore the pink-and-purple onesies with flowers and hearts that we'd already washed with baby-friendly, non-irritating laundry detergent? We kept those. But did it make sense to dress our son in the striped skirts and frilly, ruffled things that had been handed down to us by friends with older daughters? We gave those away, even though I didn't see a reason for doing so beyond the socially conditioned response that it "felt weird." Even though I knew that up until fairly recently, boys in this country wore dresses and gowns until they were five or six years old. Even though I knew that in many parts of the world, boys still wear dresses and skirts. Even though I knew that Shiv didn't care, because all he wanted at that point in his life was food, sleep, a clean butt, and cuddles.

"If we put him in that," Jill said, pointing to a small pink sundress, "he's going to hate us for it someday."

"Babe," I replied, "someday he's going to hate us anyway, no matter what we do."

But I took her point; it felt too far. To keep the less neutral, more explicitly "girl" clothes made sense in a vacuum but failed to take into consideration the world as it existed around our son. I could have pushed for a completely category- and boundaryless approach to Shiv's clothes but worried that it would be more about proving a point or performing an experiment, two things that I didn't want guiding our parenting choices. I also didn't want to have to explain my parenting philosophy and position on gender norms every time we encountered a puzzled stranger, so I let that be reason enough to get rid of the explicitly girly clothes. Still— it irked me. I felt like I was giving in. It was a feeling that would soon become familiar.

As a baby, Shiv was mistaken for a girl a few times, mostly when I was wearing him in a sling or wrap and what was visible were his chubby cheeks and mound of dark curls. I fought back my reflex to correct passing strangers when they would say, "Oh, she's beautiful!" because, you know, he *was* beautiful. And something about the urge to correct felt a little bit too much like reinforcing the notion that there is a set standard for "what a girl looks like" and "what a boy looks like." When I thought we were having a girl, I was staunchly against affixing a (sometimes alarmingly large) bow to the head of an infant, as if to clearly stake territory for the correct team, like planting a flag on the moon. *Why should it bother me if she's mistaken for a boy?* was now *So what if people think he's a girl?*

It was easy to think that when Shiv was just a baby and the lines were blurrier, when the reaction to wrong assumptions was no more than a shrug of the shoulders and a shared laugh if someone got my child's gender wrong. People desperately want to know the gender of your baby, but they usually don't go so far as to police the gender expression of that baby—after all, gender-neutral baby clothes *do* exist, a phenomenon that disappears after age one or two. With babies, there is not yet the threat of a gender-nonconforming child being seen as the reflection of a parent's moral failing, a mistake in need of correction. There is not yet the threat of violence and intimidation—verbal, psychological, physical—against those who do not play by the rules.

That threat started to creep in around the edges at age two, when Shiv went through a phase where he would ask us to paint his toes and fingernails because he saw us painting ours. (And also, let's face it, because from the perspective of a kid who loves bright colors and attention, why *wouldn't* you want to paint your nails?) Even though he was still a toddler, he encountered resistance, objections from all kinds of people in all kinds of places: our middle-aged neighbor John, who brings back gifts for Shiv whenever he goes to visit his family in China; Gloria, the security guard who sits at the entrance of Shiv's grandparents' neighborhood and who herself sports long neon acrylic nails; and the little girl at the library who asked my son, "Are you a girl?" to which he replied, "No, I a boy." "But your fingernails are painted," she insisted. "Only girls paint their fingernails." Five years old and already toeing the party line.

We're the opposite of helicopter parents when it comes to things like climbing trees, getting dirty, using knives to help make dinner, but we've been doggedly careful about whom Shiv spends his time around: the school he attends, the babysitters we employ, the friends with whom he has playdates; we can afford that luxury of choice, and we've taken full advantage. I knew all along that we could control only so much, but still, I am dazzled by how *fast* the indoctrination has happened, how futile it was to think that we would ever keep him mostly away from this stuff when it is, in fact, the water we swim in.

When I taught eighth grade, I did a unit on media and pop culture; we examined TV commercials, magazine ads, song lyrics. At the start of the unit, I divided the students by gender and asked them to construct two lists—one for the "ideal man" and one for the "ideal woman," by asking themselves, according to society, what does the ideal man or woman say, do, look like, care about, and so forth? They always worked eagerly on this task, talking excitedly in their separate groups. At the end, we compared their lists, which were, of course, basically identical. Then I would ask, "So where do you think these rules come from? Did anyone ever sit you down and tell you these things? How or when do you think you learned them?"

The ideas we inherit, the ones we construct, and what is inherently true: These are like overlapping Venn diagrams, invisible and pervasive, coloring every interaction and reaction. Is it possible to untangle them, to know what we're choosing versus what is really there? Probably not. But I still find myself wishing that as a society we could, as my students did, at least get a better look at the whole messy ball of string.

Shiv was about one month shy of turning three when he ran into my closet and declared, "I wanna wear a dress, Mama!"

"You want to wear a dress?" I echoed. He'd never expressed this desire before. I thought maybe he meant a "towel dress," which is what we call his postbath habit of asking one of us to wrap and tuck his towel around him, just under his armpits.

"You want a towel dress, baby?"

"No, not towel dress. A dress!" he insisted.

So I did what all parents and caregivers of toddlers do—I improvised. Using a tropical-patterned summer shirt I pulled from a hanger, I fashioned my son a dress. He immediately pranced to the full-length mirror to admire himself and swish around in his new attire. He was delighted.

A day before, we were shopping at Target when we went to look at their kids' shoes. Shiv's feet, it seems, are always growing, and always growing out of the shoes he already owns. As I pushed him through the narrow aisles, he pointed at a pair of *Frozen*-themed "girl shoes" and declared, "I want those." He hadn't seen the movie yet and didn't realize they were *Frozen*-themed "girl shoes," but he wanted them, probably because they had a swatch of pink and silver on them. I hesitated at his request, then was ashamed of myself for hesitating, then glanced over my shoulder to make sure there weren't fellow shoppers close by who were going to pass judgment or intervene. I looked for the shoes in his size and was relieved when there didn't seem to be any. He settled for a pair of more boring but still fairly cool-looking Shaun White–themed "boy shoes."

I hear a lot of fellow parents talk about how they "constantly" worry about their kids, worry about whether they're good parents, worry about the future, worry about bad things that could potentially happen. I don't experience that kind of worry, or I haven't yet. My anxiety tends to stem from the micro-level details rather than the big picture. On the whole, I think we're doing pretty well with this parenting thing; I don't fret about the generalities. But the specific moments, the ones where I manage to betray my deeply held values—the ones I promised myself I'd parent around—they haunt me. What kind of message am I sending? Will Shiv remember this moment? What if my momentary hesitation is what pushes him to decide to forever abandon some part of his true self-expression?

To assuage my guilt over this particular incident, I attempted to redeem myself at Old Navy a few weeks later. I was there to return a few things, and I told him we could spend the resulting store credit (about $20) on a few new things for him; he selected a Spider-Man T-shirt from the boys' section and a pair of gray flats with silver studs from the girls'.

During this time in his life, Shiv used exclusively female pronouns for everyone. When he played pretend and wanted to assume a position of power, he referred to himself as a "lady princess." He would put on a pair of my heels, throw Jill's purse over his arm, and tell us, "I going to work!" More recently, he's become obsessed with superheroes, as many boys his age do, except that he pretends to be Batgirl as often as or more than he pretends to be Batman. When Gigi offered to buy him a cape and mask to wear to my school on superhero-themed field day, he picked the pink-and-purple Spider-Girl set.

I wonder how much all of this is due to the fact that he spends the majority of his time with women: me, Jill, my mom. His teachers are all women, though he plays equally with boys and girls at school. He sees his grandfather regularly, who wrestles with him and occasionally tells him to be "tough" but also keeps his peace whenever Shiv shows up in a dress.

I've learned from many male friends (who are now men in Shiv's life, whom he does see and spend time with, just not on a daily basis) that much of this policing of gender roles is internalized by boys very early in life and passed along both as a way of enforcing one's own belonging and as a method of protecting the vulnerable. Every guy I know can pinpoint a moment when they stepped outside the boundaries of what was acceptably masculine and got quickly corrected. And that begets many years of self-censorship. Of course, women can be just as guilty and militant about enforcing men's masculinity. Jill and I have both accumulated quite the roster of attempts to get out from under our own ties to expectations of gender. She had to work to convince her parents to pay for drum lessons, even though girls "didn't play the drums" in Shreveport, Louisiana, in the 1970s (she did, and she did it better than any of the boys or men twice her age). At my childhood birthday parties, I would grin with delight whenever I'd unwrap a Barbie, not because that was what I wanted but because I knew my mom would let me return every last one of them, giving me the equivalent amount of cash to spend at the bookstore however I liked. We know what it's like to carve out room for yourself in a crowded space; we want our son to have more breathing room than we did.

Though his aesthetics tend toward the "girl" side of whatever store we happen to be in, Shiv also spends a lot of time doing things generally associated with boys: play-fighting, pretending to be a superhero, shooting water guns, wrestling, growling like a dinosaur/bear/lion, running at alarmingly fast speeds, getting dirty, talking about farts and poop. Many men I know were kicked out of the realm of princesses and playing house as boys, just as many women I know were kicked out of the trees they loved climbing or told they were no longer allowed to ride around the neighborhood shirtless. In childhood, we are permitted to blur boundaries that later get drawn with permanent-marker thickness, permitted to occupy multiple realms that we are later told are mutually exclusive.

It's cliché to say that we parents learn from our children, but Shiv has taught me to be less afraid of what others think. Because I am so invested in protecting his relatively egalitarian notions about what belongs to whom and giving his self-expression as much room as I possibly can, my own comfort level comes second. I have been scared, and scared of him seeing my fear; scared of what the checkout lady would say when he held up the Elsa costume he had asked me to buy him; scared of what would happen on the day he asked to wear that costume to school; scared of who was going to burst his beautiful bubble.

Not far behind dresses came an interest in hair, specifically long hair. Shiv started with T-shirts, which he used as a stand-in for real hair. I don't recall the exact origin of this look, but somehow he and Jill created a system where he'd wear a polo shirt on his head, the neck of the shirt snug against his actual hairline, with the rest of the shirt hanging down to his shoulders. Eventually, we bought him headbands so that he was wearing the shirts in a Lawrence of Arabia/kaffiyeh–type style. As this sartorial habit developed, it became more and more elaborate. Sometimes he wanted the sleeves of the shirt tucked in. Sometimes he wanted his "hair" in a ponytail. Sometimes he wanted to sub in other things for the T-shirt: a tutu, a stuffed octopus, a dish towel. Everything, it seemed, had the potential to be hair.

Because there is nothing one cannot purchase via Amazon Prime, Jill ordered wigs on the internet and those took over for a time as his preferred hair; he has a long black one (which he eventually asked Jill to cut short, with bangs, to match his aunt Kym), a short pink one, and a long blond Elsa wig in a braid. He is so often "wearing hair" of some kind or another that it has become routine: at home, at Target, at school, at the rodeo, at the doctor's office. It's ironic that Jill and I thought we wouldn't be "doing hair" when we found out Shiv was a boy, because we have spent all kinds of time and energy styling, restyling, locating rubber bands, and vacuuming up wig hair. For a while, Shiv became so fixated on and so particular about his hair that it led to fights and meltdowns. If we didn't get his hair *just right*, he'd freak out, or he'd change his mind about the style he wanted, asking us to re-do it over and over again. At one point, the hair situation was so intense that my mom outright banned the wigs from her house. In our house, it is considered a privilege that, like screen time, can be taken away as a consequence of unacceptable behavior.

It's common for toddlers to use whatever they can to exert control inside a life where they have very little say; we tell them where to go and when, what to eat and when, how to behave . . . so the hair, to at least some extent, seemed like a demonstration of autonomy. And as Shiv has increased his capacity for self-control and developed more and more the ability to articulate and manage his feelings, "doing his hair" is no longer equivalent with gearing up for battle.

Still, I wonder what it's all about. It's not like he's watching us do our hair; Jill and my mom both keep theirs very short, and my head is shaved, precisely because I got tired of dealing with it. He talks about hairstyles of the girls he plays with at school—*I want my hair to look like Kathryn's! Can I have a ponytail like Nedi?* He'll notice the hairstyles of strangers on playgrounds or female characters in books. Recently, we agreed to let him grow his own hair out so that more styling options would be available to him; because of his proclivity to roll around in sand and dirt, we had previously kept his hair extremely short. Now, the curls are mounding up on his head and he regards them with impatient anticipation, tolerates my scrubbing of his head in the bath because it's a condition of the grow-out-your-hair plan:

ME: Wow, bud, your curls are getting so long!

HIM: Really, really long? When are they going to be really, really long?

ME: Well, it's going to take a while, sugar, but you're getting there.

HIM: I want my hair to be really, really long, like a girl!

ME: You know, there are lots of boys and men with long hair, too.

HIM: *No!* I want my hair to be *long* like a *girl's*.

I get the sense not that Shiv wishes to be differently gendered but rather that he wants access to the trappings that society has designated as belonging to girls—long hair, dresses, ribbons, pink, sparkly things. And what if that's all there is to it? A simple aesthetic preference for long hair, nothing to understand or contextualize or try to explain. The only difficult thing about this, really, is resisting the impulse to make it mean something.

For a while, I had to deliberately cultivate an attitude of nonchalance about Shiv's hair, acting like it was nothing out of the ordinary, while daring people to say something rude so that I could educate them. But over time, my defensiveness wore away, bolstered by Shiv's complete lack of self-consciousness; if people were staring, he either didn't notice or didn't care. When strangers asked questions about his hair, I deferred to Shiv, working hard not to match their tone of amusement, tempting though it was to shrug my shoulders and employ a "kids will be kids" kind of dismissiveness. This was clearly important to him, clearly part of his self-expression, so I felt I owed him that. For his part, when questioned, he would put on his best teenager/toddler face and respond, "It's my *hair*," as if it should be obvious.

The danger of all stereotypes, of course, is that they prevent us from seeing people for who they are, in their fullness and roundness. Instead, a stereotype flattens, limits, makes the expansive small. This is part of why Jill and I have deliberately chosen to post images of Shiv on Facebook, and not just to a small, select group. Shiv clacking around in his new tap shoes on the kitchen tile; Shiv in sparkly glitter shoes; Shiv rock climbing; Shiv zooming down the Slip 'N Slide; Shiv wearing his hair and dancing to Beyoncé— all these images challenge the default assumptions about what his childhood might, or should, look like.

Because he is black, male, and big for his age, it seems our collective imagination can imagine only one thing for him: sports. And very specific kinds of sports at that. If I had a dollar for every time someone asked or implied that my son was going to play football, we could forgo the college scholarship that everyone assumes he is headed for:

Future linebacker, right here!

I'd bet you'd be great at football, buddy.

You got him in any sports yet?

We have long vowed that we would allow him to pursue his own interests, instead of "planting" or disproportionately encouraging the ones we wanted him to have. So Jill and I have made an effort to expose Shiv to a variety of activities, including sports. She and my father-in-law both watch professional sports on television; thanks to my job as a high school teacher, he's been to games of all kinds: volleyball, girls' and boys' basketball, baseball, girls' and boys' soccer, football, lacrosse. And up to this point, he has not shown any interest. He's much more interested in playing with other kids his age who happen to be in the stands, or sitting with "Mommy's students," or trying to convince me to buy him something sugary and full of artificial food coloring from the concessions stand. When we watched the Super Bowl this year at my in-laws' house, he was far more transfixed by Beyoncé's halftime show than anything else.

Conversely, Shiv's response when I've taken him to school to see various theatrical productions and performances has been exponentially more enthusiastic. He was not yet three when we went to see his babysitter Rachel in *Seussical;* I wasn't sure how he would handle a darkened theater and a prolonged period of sitting still, so we arrived after intermission to catch the second act. But as he sat enthralled, I realized that I could have easily brought him for the entire show. At three years old, he made it through the full production of *The Little Mermaid,* in which another one of his babysitters, Bram, was playing the lead role of Prince Eric. Shiv had been anxiously awaiting "the mermaid show" for weeks; months later, he still talks about it, dropping characters' names in his play-pretend, asking clarifying questions about the plot, requesting that I sing him songs from the show. I'm not sure if it's a blessing or a curse that I still know every word to "Part of Your World," but I certainly never would have thought that knowledge would come in handy when putting my four-year-old son to bed.

Shiv has likewise made it easy to follow his cues when it comes to one activity in particular: dance. Our child has been a dancer since he could walk. He has rhythm, that elusive quality easier to define by pointing out its absence. His auntie Coco, our dear friend who danced for years in her youth and is a certified dance instructor now, knew early on. "He's walking on his toes, just like I did. That's a dancer's walk."

We have video after video of Shiv dancing to every kind of music, in every kind of way, well before he could talk: high stepping, Riverdance-esque jig, hip-shaking belly dance, fluid ballerina twirls. We used our family Sabbath, which we observe on Friday nights, as an opportunity to have "music education nights," selecting an artist or genre to play for him. Jill handled funk and disco nights; I made sure that Bruce Springsteen and Led Zeppelin were represented.

One night in November, we took our dancing outside after dinner, swirling around the backyard firepit like a trio of witches in the fall darkness. One of us, I'm not sure who or why, began to sing in a fake opera voice, which two-year-old Shiv thought was delightful. "More *ooo-ooo* music!" he demanded. We went inside and I grabbed my phone—we normally turn electronics off as part of our Sabbath observance, using them only for recipes or to play music, but this felt like a reason worth breaking our tradition. For his first exposure to true opera, only the best would do, so I pulled up video of Luciano Pavarotti singing "Nessun Dorma" with the New York Philharmonic. Shiv sat in my lap, so unusually still, quiet except for his breathing, which I could hear quicken. When the aria was over, he reached down to push the play button again, and again, and again. He watched it half a dozen times.

We tried to follow his lead; I pulled up videos on YouTube that I thought he would like, regardless of whether they seemed like "kid stuff." He had the same response to the overture from the 1961 film version of *West Side Story*. He is a big fan of Broadway tap numbers; he once sat entranced before a twelve-minute video of Savion Glover improvising on a stage the size of a coffee table. When he was three, we asked him if he wanted to go to a dance class, "like Nate," referring to the book we had (blessedly!) found at our wonderful local library that tells the story of a boy (he's actually a dog—all of the characters in the book are) who loves to dance but whose brother tries to convince him that dancing is gross and only for girls. Luckily, Nate's parents are supportive and enroll him in dance class, where he loves the class but is discouraged to be the only boy; then his mom takes him to see a professional ballet in a big, fancy theater and he is so entranced by the lights and the movement that it takes him a few moments to realize that half the dancers are men. (I may or may not tear up every time I read this book aloud.) So when we asked him if he wanted to go to a dance class like Nate, Shiv said enthusiastically, "Yay-hoo!"

When his first pair of ballet shoes arrived, he twirled around, humming to himself. We did not have to explain to him what they were for or how to use them; he went up on his toes, put his arms above his head. Tap shoes were an even easier sell; they make noise. "We might regret this," I raised my eyebrows and said to Jill. "At his age, I was taking out pots and pans to bang on in order to convince my parents to sign me up for drum lessons," she replied. My mom used to pick me up from piano lessons with my dinner in the car. While I ate, she drove me to my private ice-skating lesson. It was our turn.

Finding a dance studio came with some of the same challenges as finding a school. We wanted a match in terms of ethos and approach—real teaching, not just play, but also a sense of fun and joy, not shame and competitiveness. We wanted diversity in terms of the bodies that Shiv would be surrounded by. We wanted a place that wouldn't be offended by a two-mom household. And we wanted a place that would enthusiastically welcome our dancing boy.

We feel lucky to have found Shiv's dance company; it's a wonderful community of people who are serious, but not *too* serious, about dance, who have been welcoming and friendly, quirky and warm. Each year, at the final recital, dancers of all colors, shapes, and sizes performed pieces ranging from ballet to tap to jazz to modern to hip-hop. There are easily a hundred kids who perform, and we've only ever seen one other boy. It's not that the studio doesn't want boys in their program; in fact, they offer a discount for male students, to encourage them to attend. But according to dance teachers I've spoken with, it is still rare to see boys at a dance studio unless they're waiting for their sister to finish a class. Little boys, of course, are often signed up for T-ball or soccer as a matter of default, because that's what it seems like they should do, or would want to do, or will enjoy. Likewise, girls are signed up for ballet or gymnastics, motivated by the same set of assumptions. And probably most of these kids are fine with what they are slotted into, either because they genuinely enjoy it or because they are expected to join it or because they are afraid to express an interest in something else. Or because nothing else has been presented to them.

When I first signed Shiv up, our studio director told me that most boys don't come to dance until they are older—until they have convinced their parents that they really don't want to play a sport with a ball or a bat, that they really want to dance. "And then, of course, it is harder to keep the boys around, because the older they are, the more self-conscious they tend to get, the more teasing they may receive."

Clothing is always an issue in social situations, since it serves as shorthand for specialness and belonging. For his weekly dance class, Shiv wears leggings and snug athletic T-shirts that I find in the girls' section (good luck finding dance clothes cut for boys who occupy the ninety-ninth percentiles for height and weight), plus his black ballet shoes or tap shoes. The girls in his class wear exactly what you'd expect little girls in a ballet class to wear—pink or black leotards with tutus, plus tights. Same shoes as Shiv, except their ballet slippers are pink. It never seems to bother him.

Preparations for his first recital began a full five months

before the actual performance, because we're talking about teaching two- and three-year-olds a three-minute dance routine. As the only boy, Shiv was slotted into a special piece of choreography: the routine began with him leaping across a line of pliéing girls, handing a flower to each one before joining them at the end of the line. From there, all of the kids did the same moves, some cute pantomiming and lots of twirling. It was totally adorable, and totally gendered, but we didn't want to pick a fight about it.

Then the costumes arrived. All of the kids had been measured during class a few weeks prior, but we weren't told what the outfits would look like. On the day the kids were trying their outfits on, I was rushing to meet up with Jill at the dance studio for a child handoff when I received a series of text messages from her:

> He's upset that he doesn't have a tutu like the girls. He won't do the routine. :(

> Ok. We're going to have to talk to him. He is steadfastly refusing to dance and he looks so sad. He feels left out because he didn't get a dress like the girls. He got a lace-up tunic.

This dance costume snafu was easily solved by a quick conversation with his teachers; they were happy for us to take Shiv's costume and "bling it up," in the words of one of our fellow dance moms—all of whom were, to their credit, completely sympathetic with his desire for a fancy outfit. As she often does, Auntie Coco came to the rescue, sewing gold rickrack around the shirt's collar, adding two spectacular gold-sequined ruffles to the bottom, and affixing gold sequins to the sleeves with hot glue. The boy was thrilled.

A few months prior, Shiv had worn a tutu in public for the first time: to see *The Nutcracker,* also for the first time. As I helped him get dressed for the evening, he asked if he could wear his tutu over his pants, and I said, "Of course." He got a few shy compliments and lots of smiles. It was mostly, though not all, a white audience, and I thought a lot about the importance of people seeing my black son in a tutu, of what his presence creates and makes possible. Patrisse Cullors, one of the founders of the Black Lives Matter movement, argues that, as a society, "we've forgotten how to imagine black life. . . . That's our collective imagination. Someone imagined handcuffs; someone imagined guns; someone imagined a jail cell. Well, how do we imagine something different that actually centers black people, that sees them in the future? Let's imagine something different."

The morning before Shiv's dance recital dress rehearsal, he and I set off on an adventure with the dog, tromping around the backyard lake in the mud and muck, him getting wet up to his bottom in lake water, running, carrying sticks, both of us pretending to be superheroes with magic powers. And then the same boy, with the same level of excitement, took a shower, got dressed up in his leggings and ballet shoes, sat perfectly still while I put makeup on him for the first time, smoothing on his foundation and lining his eyes with my black pencil, teaching him to press his lips together in a kiss to blot the lipstick I applied. He took one look in the mirror and told me, "I'm pretty, Mama!"

You are, my boy. You are.

Pretending to Be White

My hometown is a southern city with demographics that reflect generations of gerrymandering, white flight, and other forms of racist violence generated by fears of integration. According to a 2017 study, Memphis is the fourth most segregated city in the nation. Even as a child, it was always clear to me that the city was zoned (both officially and unofficially) into black and white—I was raised with clear knowledge of which neighborhoods were the "bad" ones. Because of Memphis's high crime rate, conversation was often framed around concerns for "safety," never directly alluding to race. I internalized directions and landmarks, only later understanding their full significance—*we always take a right onto Highland off Park because otherwise you drive into Orange Mound; Mendenhall becomes Mt. Moriah, and once the name changes, it's no longer a good place to be.* These rules were mostly unspoken but effectively conveyed all the same. In my hometown, race is a constant undercurrent.

Growing up in Memphis was a mixed bag when it came to the extent to which any of this was discussed outright. Though the city has a unique role in American history, which we were taught, there was virtually no attempt to connect the happenings in Memphis's past with any of the race-related issues facing the city or the country in the present day. We all knew what had happened at the Lorraine Motel in 1968, knew that the lyrics in the U2 song were wrong (Dr. King was assassinated in the early evening, not the "early morning"). But at my almost exclusively white private school, we had little idea of just how much we didn't know. I received what would be considered by nearly every standard an exemplary education, and what I was taught about race in America was slavery and the civil rights movement and that was about it. I remember watching *Eyes on the Prize* but can't think of a single book I was assigned to read in twelve years by an author who wasn't white. The overarching message was that race was an issue of the past, something our society had overcome but that no longer played a part in our everyday lives.

I say "our" because I grew up surrounded by whiteness to such an extent that I would, at times, think of myself as belonging to it. I was afforded a very intimate look at a particular kind of whiteness, wealthy and well established and sanctimonious. The whiteness I came to know surrounded itself like a cloak to keep out the cold or a curtain drawn around a hospital bedside, refusing to look at who or what else shared the room. It often struck me as a kind of fantasyland, this exaggerated white world, with its country clubs and Derby Parties and Cotton Carnival, its fancy neighborhoods and preppy clothes, its monogrammed everything. Even in the case of white families who were somewhat liberal and considered themselves "progressive," black people entered the equation only if they were useful in some way: nannies, maids, gardeners. It was an entire posture of separateness, a code that could be violated in only one direction. White businessmen could visit soul food restaurants, tucking in their ties and digging into plates of food they could not get from any white cook, but black people only ever showed up in "white" restaurants as employees. White teenagers could joke about "slumming it" when visiting gas stations in black neighborhoods, where they thought the likelihood of being able to buy beer with a fake ID was higher, but anyone black who drove around in my neighborhood of Germantown seemed to invariably get pulled over, often on the falsest of pretenses.

As a brown girl growing up in a black-and-white context, I automatically paid attention to the seemingly contradictory power dynamics that ruled my every day—white people held political and fiscal sway, but black people possessed cultural power that drew white attention. From music to food to the history Memphis is famous for, everything that made the city a draw came either directly or obliquely through black folks: even Elvis, whose figure casts a seemingly interminable shadow over the life of every Memphian, owed his career to the fact that he was a white guy who "dared" to appropriate black sound and style. (One might say the same about the city's most famous living pop star, Justin Timberlake.) Even now, the things that white Memphians seem to brag about, everything the city's tourism bureau develops its ad campaigns around—including the slogan of the city's NBA team, the Grizzlies' "Grit & Grind," and the ubiquitous boast that Memphis has "soul"—has very little to do with the white people who claim or tout it.

For a long time, I had no idea that there was anything particularly unique about growing up in Memphis. But once I got to college and started comparing stories with new friends, I realized that I'd had many idiosyncratic experiences that weren't shared by others who were raised elsewhere and began to wonder how formative these experiences might have been. The public park closest to my childhood home is on the National Register of Historic

Places; it preserves what's left of a fort built by Union troops during the Civil War. I thought nothing of climbing on the replica cannons when I was a kid or of the reenactors who would show up there in the summers. One of my elementary school friends' houses was so old there were still quarters in the backyard that had once housed servants. In her dining room, a button on the floor allowed the mistress of the house to ring a bell in the kitchen and summon "the help." Two miles away from the National Civil Rights Museum, built on the site of the Lorraine Motel, where Martin Luther King Jr. was shot, was a park that featured, until just a few months ago, an enormous statue of Nathan Bedford Forrest, early leader of the Ku Klux Klan and prolific slave trader.

When I was growing up in Memphis, the prevailing attitude around racial injustice as an issue or topic for discussion inside the affluent white communities I knew was a kind of syrupy sympathy, a sort of tongue-clucking—*Isn't that a shame*—that abdicated the speaker and their community from being in any way complicit or responsible for the way things were. The problem was never racism, of course, it was poverty or drugs or crime, it was teen pregnancy, it was absentee parents, it was dozens of different euphemisms that all managed to talk about the same thing without ever naming it directly. These "good white people" traveled in entirely white social circles, had exclusively white friends, and would deny, vehemently, that they were in any way racist. (I grew to chafe under that delightful chestnut used in reference to Memphis's black community, *Well, they're racist, too, you know*.)

I grew accustomed to, dare I say comfortable with, this kind of whiteness, though one never feels a hundred percent comfortable being the only non-white face in the room. More often, I was the only non-white non-employee. My wealthier friends had nannies or maids, and they were always black; at weddings or birthday parties at country clubs, I would feel my guilt bloom under the gaze of the dress-shirt-clad waiters and waitresses loading sheet pans into steam trays, while I felt the need to account for my presence. Though I did not quite have the words for what it was, it seemed that I was betraying something by standing on the other side of the table. My coping mechanism at the time was to disassociate, to try to escape my discomfort; I smiled politely, said *thank you,* did everything I could to feign obliviousness to the strangeness of the situation.

Growing up comfortable in the presence of white people necessarily meant that I felt uncomfortable in the presence of black people. Though my family had plenty of brown friends, we, like the white people we knew, did not have any black ones. There were even fewer black girls at my school than there were Indian ones, and even though I was friends with some of them, we never spoke about or related our experiences vis-à-vis the whiteness that surrounded us. For my part, to have a chance of thriving in that environment meant being very careful about drawing attention to my not-whiteness; it was one thing to be celebrated for the "diversity" I brought to campus, but quite another to utilize my otherness as a place from which to criticize. I had too much good immigrant girl training to even let myself think about the things I wished my alma mater did differently or better until after I had graduated from it.

My primary first-person exposure to blackness was through my parents' workplaces. Both my mother, who was a special education teacher, and my father, who managed the production plant for a local restaurant group, worked in majority-black environments, and I never quite knew how to behave when I visited them at work. I felt shy, and conspicuous, and uncertain how to relate; each of my parents had black co-workers with whom they had extremely positive working relationships and black co-workers with whom they struggled. These differences were not solely based on race, but they weren't separate from racial dynamics either. Though I was young, I was still aware that power was in play since my parents served in supervisory roles, had more formal education, and were better compensated than their black colleagues. What I didn't know much about was colorism, or that it existed in the black community in ways not dissimilar from what I had encountered in India. The difference was, of course, that I seemed dark to my Indian relatives but light to many of the black women my parents worked with, who made me uncomfortable when they told me I had pretty skin.

Spending time at work with my parents gave me exposure—albeit limited—to a world I found engaging but where I did not think I belonged. I loved the easy laughter of the women who worked in special ed classrooms with my mom, loved the food that the employees my father supervised sent home around the holidays. I developed an ear for the cadence of African American vernacular English, sounds that grew to feel familiar and that I never had trouble deciphering, but that I didn't dare attempt to speak back. For one thing, I wasn't sure it would be allowed, and I also wasn't sure that I wanted to. My nascent sense of who held what kind of power encouraged me to ally myself with and imitate the white people I went to school with and not the black people my parents worked with. All the white people I knew were affluent; the poverty I saw in Memphis was always black in color. Memphis is a poor city overall, with a poverty rate close to thirty percent, but when you break it down by race, the numbers speak volumes—twice as many black Memphians live in poverty as their white counterparts. Though I had been exposed to middle-class and upper-class black families through girls I knew from school (and, let's face it, on *The Cosby Show*), I saw them the way that white people saw me: as the exception.

For a long time, I did a pretty good imitation of a white girl; I embraced being the model minority without realizing that's what I was doing. My standards and expectations for how to be, how to conduct myself, what to aspire to: These were primarily based on the white examples around me. I never aspired to assimilate fully—perhaps because I did not think such a thing possible— but I was still reticent about my difference, wary of being lumped into a large category of non-white "others." I didn't realize that it might be problematic to embrace white people's tendency to think of me as exotic, or that their propensity for appropriating my culture was something I could object to; to me, making allowances for these happenings seemed like my main way "in," a way that would allow me to still be different, but the good kind of different.

Internalizing the tastes and manners of the white culture that surrounded me felt key to my survival because of the limited representations to which I had access. The options for what it meant to be brown, as far as I could tell, were to be black or be white, a set of options that barely even registered as a choice. My friends called me "brownest white girl"—a label I find incredibly troubling now but that I once carried proudly, like a trophy. I now know that this "exceptionalism," particularly as it's ascribed to Asian Americans, has historically been used as a wedge between minority groups, keeping them fractured and distrustful of one another. But I didn't see any of that growing up. I thought I could perform whiteness without absorbing all of the attendant bias.

I grew up idolizing the very lifestyles I also resented, unconsciously setting them as the bar for what a positive future would look like. These ideas were undoubtedly reinforced by my parents and the immigrant community we were a part of; while our parents held on to certain Indian value systems, like those related to their religious observance and their sense of family, they also took on many of the cultural norms and values of their adopted home: celebrating Thanksgiving, embracing the great American road trip, proudly flying the flag on the Fourth of July—things for which they had no prior frame of reference. In much the same way, though we were not white, we framed what we *were* the same way whiteness originally created itself—in opposition to blackness.

Our parents bought into the dream of this country and, like new converts, fed it zealously to us: opportunity, privilege, responsibility, success. That dream, of course, was modeled on a conventional American understanding of what success "looks like," meaning it was modeled on straight, wealthy white people. For our parents, success looked like graduate degrees (law school or medical school—business school was acceptable but not quite as good), it looked like money, it looked like heterosexual marriage and kids and a nice house in a "good" part of town. Our parents were willing to make concessions—they conceded the possibility of some of us marrying white guys, allowed us to date, to cut our hair short, to go to prom. But there were always limits, laid out jokingly, but not jokes at all. *Just don't bring a black boy home . . . or a Muslim boy.* One of these prejudices immigrated with our parents across the ocean; the other, they absorbed. It was in the water everywhere around us, that Memphis water people claim has a distinctive taste. How could we not have taken it in osmotically, through the skin? We thought we were observing the two worlds from a distance, occasionally dropping in as visitors or guests, but we weren't, of course. We were participants. We were complicit.

For years, I felt no solidarity with other people of color—in fact, I tended to avoid them, particularly if they seemed politically charged or willing to wave their race or ethnic identity flag more enthusiastically than I thought necessary. I cringe now when I remember how many times I felt relief that I was the "right" kind of immigrant because my parents had come here legally and basked in the attention that came with being the kind of immigrant success story people like to trot out. Back then, I had very little knowledge of how the immigration system worked, knew nothing about quotas or measures of worthiness or how much luck played a part in my parents making it here. I had no sense of history, no knowledge that my people—like nearly every group of people before us—hadn't always been welcomed here the way that history textbooks and talk of "melting pots" made it seem. I remain proud of my parents, who did, in fact, work incredibly hard to build the life I came to take for granted. But what my family and I didn't see, as so many white Americans don't, were the systems of privilege and structural advantages that contributed to our success. And that by accepting the Dream, we also accepted the rest of the narrative. We didn't read the fine print.

We thought that we were progressive—at least, it seemed like we were. Election year after election year, we continued to be one of the rare front yards in Germantown *not* sporting a sign for the Republican candidate du jour; I was one of a handful of kids at my elite private middle school who proudly sported a pin for Clinton-Gore on my jean jacket. My parents listened to NPR and watched *The NewsHour with Jim Lehrer;* my mother made it a point to explain why they voted for candidates even when it meant tax increases for our family; they were happy to pay, felt that doing so was fair, part of what came with being financially successful, a willingness to share with others for the benefit of everyone.

And we did talk about race. As brown people existing in a city that was starkly divided between black and white, it would have been impossible to claim we "didn't see color." The attempts of others to categorize or place us into proper context went a long way toward teaching us about the way race worked in America. Though we faced ignorance and discrimination (my parents more so than I), we were regarded with a kind of curious fascination, often annoying but mostly well meaning. As Indians with brown skin, we did not rank on the social ladder with our friends and neighbors with white skin, but we were also saved from the bottom of that ladder because we had money and because we were not black. This is what activist Deepa Iyer has termed the "racial bribe": access to higher status for immigrants who carry the party line, which includes regarding blacks as inferior. Though it seems obvious to me now, for so long I was ignorant—probably willfully so—of the extent to which my parents and I and our immigrant community had internalized the dominant narrative around race. Even though we of all people ought to have known better, ought to have seen. But, as Nobel Prize–winning author Toni Morrison says, "Whatever the ethnicity or nationality of the immigrant, his nemesis is understood to be African American."

The racism I witnessed within the immigrant community I grew up in mirrored what I saw in the white communities I spent time in: it was covert, coded, subtle. References to *those people* coupled with the tendency to shift the conversation to the black community's own responsibility for their problems are what stand out in my mind, though it's possible that I heard uglier things that either didn't register or I don't remember. Within our Indian community, my family was on the liberal end of the spectrum, so it was common to hear conservative talk that I knew my parents disagreed with; my mom was notorious for engaging in political debates, my dad more likely to gloss over differences so as not to ruin the good time everyone was having.

These days, I occupy so many different societal intersections that my tether of belonging to the community that raised me feels tenuous, still valid only by virtue of being grandfathered in. I feel cut or impacted by many different events, but my community doesn't necessarily have the same experience or recognize that my experience is different from theirs. In 2015, one of my aunties circulated a petition about Sureshbhai Patel, the Indian grandfather who was attacked by Alabama police while walking around his family's neighborhood. As a recipient of the e-mail, I was also subject to a series of "reply all" outcries and demands for justice, none of which I disagreed with; this incident, like all examples of police brutality, was horrifying. But where were these people when twelve-year-old Tamir Rice, whom my son will someday resemble, was gunned down in a public park by the police?

Becoming the parent of a black son has given me the perspective to see that there is a real reluctance to engage in a conversation about the Asian American community's participation in anti-black racism. Related to this is a tendency to accommodate and apologize; I learned early on that white people are bad at being uncomfortable, so in order to deal with them successfully, you have to give them the benefit of the doubt, cut them slack, and not make too much of a big deal about anything. But I am no longer willing to inconvenience myself or make parts of myself invisible so that I don't upset others—whether they're white people or brown people.

As a college student, I developed an awareness that I had taken on the tastes and aesthetics of the white world inside which I was raised, but the biases that came along with that inheritance remained hidden to me for many years. Then, the summer before my senior year of college, I landed an internship on Capitol Hill. It wasn't glamorous (if any of these internships ever are); the small, bipartisan commission for which I'd be working consisted of a staff of twenty and had zero name recognition among the general public. Still, I was getting the chance to spend a summer in D.C., and I was thrilled. My parents generously offered to cover my expenses and helped me find a room to sublet in a three-bedroom apartment in Columbia Heights.

At that time, Columbia Heights was considered a "transitional" neighborhood: another one of those coded words that really means "not many white people live here." The neighborhood had gone from being at the top of the list of places tourists should never visit to the top of the list of the District's prime targets for gentrification. When Metrorail's green line expanded north, Columbia Heights got a subway station of its own, bringing commerce in the form of local businesses: hair braiding, discount furniture, Laundromats. A bank reopened, bringing its stately, Corinthian-style building back to life, while adding bars to the bright glass windows. On my walk to the Metro every morning, I would see contractors adding crown molding and hardwood floors to the old brick town homes, anticipating the advent of higher rents. Gang graffiti was replaced with murals painted in the same style— vibrant, neon colors celebrating community, diversity, and peace. It was in Columbia Heights that I had my first taste of Salvadoran food from a small basement restaurant and learned to identify the flags of Vietnam and Somalia that flew high above the tiny backyard gardens of refugees.

Even though the demographics of D.C. are very much in line with my hometown, when I first arrived in Columbia Heights, I felt certain that I didn't belong. On the cab ride there, I despaired when my driver flew past the trendy neighborhoods with their familiar boutiques and coffee shops, only to come to a stop in front of a tiny corner store, its glass windows obscured by vertical stripes of metal. A lone neon sign—"BEER"—proudly declared the nature of the business. The door to my apartment was set into a wall of concrete, the paint peeling and the lobby it opened onto dank and featuring a neglected smoke alarm that beeped routinely, pleading for a new battery. Everything about the place felt shabby and unsafe. Nearly every face I saw in my new neighborhood was black or brown, and it made me incredibly uncomfortable.

I had spent my whole life in a "nice" neighborhood. When I was eighteen months old, my parents had a house built in Germantown, a small suburb of Memphis with a population at that time of about twenty thousand. Aesthetically pleasing, with perfectly manicured lawns, big brick houses, and meticulous zoning, Germantown has the lowest crime rate of any city its size in the entire state of Tennessee, its own highly ranked school district, and all the status markers my immigrant parents worked so hard to achieve. It was, in short, full of rich white people.

That was the milieu I felt comfortable with, was accustomed to, and, if I'm being completely honest, felt I deserved. I had grown up with the cognitive dissonance of knowing that I wasn't white while also sometimes forgetting that I was brown. I had all the status markers, things that my parents had hoped for and worked hard to give me: family vacations, disposable income, clothes from Gap, luxury cars, my own telephone line. At the same time, I had internalized everything that whiteness taught me to believe and feel about blackness—namely, fear. My parents managed to make it out of India, but that didn't keep us all from becoming colonized.

I had longed for the ease of moving around in the world that my white classmates seemed to have, and I thought that by imitating them, I would achieve the same. But this sword turned out to be double-edged: although it precluded a sense of belonging with other people of color, it guaranteed affinity with whiteness only up to a certain point. Something always happens to make the bubble burst—the *No, where are you* really *from?* questions, the boss who laments that he can't get the "smell of Indian food" out of his clothes, as if that food is a monolith and all of it stinks. Even though I lived inside of a white world, I was well aware that I was a visitor inside of it, granted a visa that could be revoked at any time. Reminded, time and again, like each time I was "randomly selected" for special screening at the airport, that my status was only probationary—that I could exemplify the Dream all I wanted, but at the end of the day, my skin would still be brown.

That summer in D.C. was filled with a great deal of learning for me, the kind that brings painful self-awareness with it. At first, I avoided my Columbia Heights neighborhood, returning to my apartment only to sleep, spending my time in the "hip" neighborhoods whose demographics were much more in line with what I'd grown up in (that is, mostly white). But after a few weeks, I began to steal glances at what I'd been avoiding, the way I'd check for monsters in my room as a kid by opening one eye at a time. I started to tell the truth to myself: *You don't like it here because you are unbelievably spoiled. All these black and brown people make you uncomfortable even though you are a brown person yourself.* Even then, it seemed ridiculous that I should have to remind myself of the color of my skin, but I'd spent so much time trying to fit into the company of whites that without the presence of whiteness to remind me of my brownness, I'd defaulted to a crude form of self-protection: thinking of myself as white.

There is no beautiful story that I can trot out to tie a big, shiny bow on this summer of personal realization, no heartwarming aha moment. I tried to craft one in graduate school, and my professor and several classmates called me out, further evidence that these kinds of shifts are ongoing, the work of continued pushing and awareness, not a "one and done" epiphany. Yes, I began shopping at the local grocery store instead of taking the train to Whole Foods; yes, I became friendly with some of the neighbors who would greet me as I walked to and from the Metro. But what really happened that summer was that I began the very long process of learning how to fully live inside of my brown skin, a process in which I am very much still engaged. My assumption had been that my internship would teach me all kinds of things, but in the end, it was my neighborhood that did.

(Not) Passing

On a Saturday morning in July, just a few weeks before he would turn five, Shiv told me that he "actually wasn't born a boy." We were minutes away from leaving the house, on our way to meet friends for a children's theater production of *The Wizard of Oz;* Shiv had gotten himself dressed first (in shorts and a T-shirt), but when I walked out of my bedroom wearing a sundress, he asked, "Can I wear a dress, too?"

This in and of itself was not unusual—for years, Shiv has shown an interest in dresses, wigs, dolls, and other items traditionally marked as being "for girls." But he demonstrated this interest while also identifying as a boy. While he would often play-pretend as a girl (usually some kind of superhero), he had never before shared anything that indicated he experienced himself as female on the inside. And because his exterior expression ran the gamut, my wife and I were purposeful not to assume that his interest in and enjoyment of "girl things" necessarily corresponded to Shiv being gendered differently. Except now he seemed to be introducing the possibility.

"I'm actually a girl. So please don't say 'yes sir' to me." He spoke as if testing out the idea, running it by me to see how I would respond.

"Okay," I said in what I hoped was an even, neutral tone, buying time as I helped him slip on his own sundress, thinking carefully about how to respond. *He's making a request, asking for what he needs. That's a good thing, it means he feels empowered to do that. I need to show support, not argue or contradict. Maybe ask for clarification?*

"So, no more saying 'yes sir.' But can we still use your name? Is it okay to keep calling you Shiv?"

He thought for a split second, then nodded while answering, "Yes!" Before I could take the conversation any further, Shiv and his attention bounced away from me and into the kitchen, where he proceeded to check himself out in the mirror. Reeling slightly but not wanting it to show, I took a deep breath and packed up my purse, pausing to text my friend Holly; we were on our way to meet up with her and her three sons. Shiv had played at their house several times, but always while wearing his "boy" clothes. I knew he was slightly nervous to wear a dress around them for the first time, so we rehearsed his standard response to questions or comments—*It's my choice to wear a dress and I like it*—and I also promised him I'd give Holly a heads-up. I had no doubt she would be supportive and that the boys would follow her lead, but like all kids, they swim around in the same expectation-filled water as everyone else, the water inside which no one would bat an eye at me showing up to the theater in a dress but would goggle when Shiv did.

Shiv has always had strong opinions about his personal style. He asked to wear a dress when he was one month shy of his third birthday and began wearing a T-shirt on his head (declaring that it was his "hair") around the same time. What first seemed like a quirk or a phase to Jill and me has evolved in our parental understanding into something more significant; accordingly, we have worked to give Shiv a good measure of freedom and autonomy in how he dresses and in his diva-esque aspirations. We both had parents—her mom, my dad—who either objected to or attempted to control our appearance (for her, clothes and for me, hair) and because of those sour memories are committed to not doing the same.

We have set a few limits: certain clothes are reserved for special occasions ("no wearing fancy dresses to school") and sometimes, practical logistics overrule aesthetic considerations—"no wigs in the shower or pool." Jill and I often check with each other to make sure that the limitations we're imposing have a logical and not emotional basis. Do we have a genuinely good reason for this restriction? Would we be implementing this rule if our child were a girl? Are we trying to codify something simply to reduce hassle, or to protect Shiv, and is either one of those necessarily a bad thing?

For instance: I work out at the gym about three or four times a week, and since Shiv was about eight months old, I've taken him with me. The kids' club there is cheap and convenient and has exposed him to more cartoon movies than I previously knew even existed. Thankfully, Shiv generally spends his time there clambering around the play structure or joining in the antics of whoever else happens to be there. From the start, I instituted a rule: No "hair" in the kids' club. By now it's standard procedure. Shiv removes his shirt hair in the car before we go inside the gym; then I help him put it back on when we return to the car. I've always claimed this had a practical motive—*Oh, it'll come off while you're playing and I won't be there to fix it for you*—but the truth is that I was worried he would be made fun of and I wouldn't be there to back him up. It's one thing for Shiv to dress unusually when Jill or I can be with him, or even when he's at his school, which we chose precisely because it is such an open, supportive environment. But leaving him with a group of kids I don't know, without any confidence in the willingness of the kids' club attendants (usually in their early twenties, with various levels of enthusiasm for supervising small children) to intervene on his behalf, feels entirely different. Now that he's five, I think he could handle whatever talk might come his way, but when he was a three-year-old, I just couldn't bring myself to do it. So I created a rule designed to protect him. That's what parents do, right? Then why do I feel so conflicted about it?

Shiv is old enough to know the "rules" of gender conformity, to have internalized the codes even though we routinely remind him that in our family we don't believe in them. Still, he occasionally trots out some maxim he's heard from who-knows-where: *Girls can't do that!* or *That's only for boys!* Kids his age are committed to absolutes, understanding the world in black and white, but ironically, Shiv's own self-expression demonstrates that there's a whole lotta gray. Whenever he parrots out one of these conventional gender stereotypes, it's almost as if he expects us to contradict him, and wants us to. *Remind me again that this isn't the truth. Reassure me there's another way.*

Kids push boundaries, both to assert independence and to understand where the limits are—or, in Shiv's case, to make their own limits. So far, Shiv has made his wardrobe choices based on a combination of pride and pragmatism, with a blazing certainty about what he wants and what makes him feel good. A few weeks ago, getting dressed for school, he picked out a sleeveless pink shirt with fringe and silver writing on it, plus blue shirt hair and a bright blue pair of shorts. That afternoon, I needed to run an errand after picking him up from school, and he walked right into Home Depot holding my hand without any sense that we were entering a mainstay of binary, gendered, mainstream American culture. Even though half of the customers at Home Depot (and its rival, Lowe's) are women, I still always feel that I don't belong there, like the male contractors and employees are looking at me with a kind of patronizing skepticism, prepared to jump in and mansplain home improvement to me. But Shiv comes with no such baggage; I am routinely awed by his lack of self-consciousness.

Still, there are times when others get to him or when he alters his appearance in anticipation of being laughed at. This seems to be happening more frequently as he gets older, perhaps because he is noticing things he didn't always notice before. Recently, we were leaving the park holding hands and walked past a group of kids sitting at picnic tables. As we passed by, Shiv turned his head back, finally asking me when we got to our car: "Why that boy lookin' at me like that?"

Shiv was wearing shorts, a T-shirt, shirt hair, and a pink tutu over his shorts; the boy in question, who looked to be about ten years old, was, in fact, staring at Shiv, and not in a friendly way. There was a part of me that was tempted to tell Shiv, *Oh, he's looking at you because your outfit is so cool! He's probably just jealous!* But then I thought about my own experiences being stared at as a kid because of my skin color. I thought about adults telling me I was imagining things or insisting that looks from others were positive or neutral, even though intuitively I knew that they weren't.

Don't dismiss his experience, I admonished myself. *And don't try to fix it.* Instead, I asked him a question. "How did it make you feel for that boy to look at you like that?"

"Sad," he said.

"I'm sorry, buddy. I understand why you felt sad. Sometimes people look at me funny because of my hair, because they aren't used to seeing a woman with a shaved head, and sometimes it makes me feel angry."

"What do you do?"

"Well, I try to remember that I feel good about my hair, that I like it the way it is, and that's what matters. Do you feel good about your outfit?"

"Yes."

"Then that's what's most important. And Mommy supports you no matter what."

Was it enough? I'm never sure. How to explain to a five-year-old that some people view others violating social norms as a personal affront? How to explain that Shiv pushes the buttons of those who have forgotten that these norms were constructed and not handed down from on high? How to tell him that there probably *is* an element of jealousy involved, a kind of envy at the bravery it takes to cross the lines? I think of my friend Christian, admitting that despite being a committed ally who chose to go to Pride with his wife, he still felt super uncomfortable with the guy standing nearby in a thong.

Most days, Shiv matches and resembles so much of what people (mostly moms) seem to be referring to when they use the hashtags #allboy or #suchaboy. For one thing, he looks the part: physically sturdy and broad shouldered, with thick, muscular thighs. He howls with laughter when he farts during a quiet family moment and thinks the word "poop" is hilarious. He prefers peeing outside to peeing in the toilet. His feet stink, he eats more food during a growth spurt than seems either healthy or humanly possible, and he has the ability to turn nearly any household object into an imaginary weapon of some sort. For the last year-plus, he's been obsessed with superheroes and comic book characters; Jill and I are often conscripted into *Let's go get the bad guys!* play-pretend.

Accordingly, Jill has perfected the art of making toy swords and nunchucks (which Shiv, for a time, called "nutchucks," a misnomer so delightful we decided not to correct it) out of paper towel rolls, newspaper, a roll of kitchen twine, and duct tape. Yesterday, he greeted us at breakfast by yelling in his grumpiest voice, "Ugh, my bathroom smells like *vagina!*" probably because I'd just thrown a tampon away in there. In short, he can be *such* a dude.

And yet I spent at least an hour that same day constructing dress-up outfits according to Shiv's specifications: wrapping a gauzy pink scarf around his body to make the strapless dress he had requested, thanking my years of sari-wearing experience for teaching me how to fold and pleat fabric and also how to open a safety pin with my mouth. (Attempt at your own risk.) From there, I was conscripted to construct a "veil, like a lady wears at a wedding" using another scarf, this one bright blue with a copper pattern and beaded edge. Once satisfied, Shiv walked slowly around the house, the long train dragging behind him on the floor. An hour or so later, the strapless dress had morphed into a pink-scarf skirt to which Shiv had added an old bikini top of mine, with the veil still going strong. Thusly dressed, he helped me make the icing for Jill's birthday cake.

Shiv seems to know, intuitively, that gender is performative. He occupies different incarnations of himself at different times—naming him after a Hindu god has proved appropriate. He's learned to code-switch gender markers without being explicitly instructed to do so. At times, he's so insistent on wearing a dress or a skirt, so fixated on how his hair looks, and other times he's perfectly happy to throw on a T-shirt and baggy athletic shorts. I can't track his choices, nor do I suppose I need to, but I am curious. Is he calculating potential hassle? Deciding it's not worth the risk? Or am I attributing causality where there is none?

It's been a month since Shiv's declaration that he is "actually a girl," and I feel like I've been on heightened alert. Is it the fact that I'm paying closer attention, or is it because of the culture's larger conversation around transgender rights, transphobia, and bathrooms? It's like learning a new word and then hearing it wherever you go. I'm not asserting that Shiv is transgender or will identify that way; I will wait for him to articulate his own sense of who he is. But considering the cues he's offered so far (cues that have not, up to this point, included a request for a shift in the pronouns used to refer to him), this is no phase—I am the parent of a gendernonconforming child. And because he is black, Shiv will be more susceptible to misconceptions, prejudice, and violence than a white child in the same position. With that knowledge, I have to fight against my instinct to move immediately into fear or despair. *Look at how hostile the territory is! Think how hard it will be for him!*

That kind of parental panic is something I'd previously experienced only from a child's perspective: as immigrants, my parents came with an extra layer of uncertainty and concern about the world I was being raised in. Add to that the fact that I am an only child, and you can appreciate the weight of parental expectation I carried on my shoulders. By and large, I met or exceeded the expectations my parents had for me, until, in one very distinct way, I failed. Recently, I came across a copy of a multipage, handwritten letter that my father sent me in college. He mailed me the original, but I didn't keep it; as far as letters go, this one was a decidedly unpleasant read. But apparently he made a copy of the letter before sending it, which my mom discovered in a drawer after he died. I have lots of letters and cards from him, sweet ones—birthday cards, letters he sent to me at summer camp—and I look at those from time to time. But the copy of this letter, the Letter, I keep only out of my commitment to maintaining a personal archive.

The letter is essentially a plea to "make a different choice" when it came to my "lifestyle," my father's last-ditch attempt to convince me that it wasn't too late to settle down, marry some nice man, and have a couple kids. His disappointment and shame are palpable; he could not understand why I was "doing this" to my parents, why I would opt to make all our lives "so difficult." With his words, he laid out a choice, although not the one he was referring to; the choice was about which I would put first, my true self or my relationship with my parents, particularly my dad. (My mother was also upset about my sexuality, but she did not draw such a hard line.) I had not wanted to make that choice, but his letter forced my hand. There was no question of abandoning my life with Jill or the sense of self I'd worked so hard to discover. That letter created a deep rift between my father and me, which did not fully heal before his sudden death several years later.

I still find it painful to read, as I tend to focus on the best parts of my father as I grieve for him; it is hurtful to remember this self-ish and manipulative side of him, this moment when his love became conditional. My father was a wonderful man, someone whom I love and miss tremendously, but he screwed up here. And now I am desperate to make sure that my fear or selfishness or sense of *wouldn't it just be easier if . . . ?* does not allow me to make the same mistake with my child. My desperation pushes me to hold my head higher, to fight against my upbringing as the good immigrant daughter who was taught not to take up too much space, not to make myself any more conspicuous than I already was. Rather than urging Shiv to be more cautious, I hope that being his mama makes me more brave.

I seek out books when I need guidance, and in the past few weeks I have been more grateful than ever for my public library and the internet. I've purchased *Who Am I?*, a book for kids that nicely explains the distinction between gender and sex, and *Gender Born, Gender Made,* a book for parents and caregivers, with case studies and clinical data. I deliberately left these books out around our house on the day of Shiv's birthday party, knowing that about a dozen kids and their parents would be coming over for homemade sno-cones and a backyard bounce house. The books served as a kind of litmus test, helping me see how the people in Shiv's life were likely to respond to his developing sense of identity. Jill and I agree: we cannot make the world safe, but we can make our home safe and insist that anyone who comes into it is supportive of his choices, whatever they may be.

Because what's considered permissible now for Shiv, what's seen as cute and funny, will change, and rapidly, especially because of his size. Shiv is big for his age—to the point that it's one of the first observations people make about him. As I'm writing this, he has been five for less than a month but is already the height of an average eight-year-old boy and weighs enough that his allergy doctor just upgraded him to an adult EpiPen from an EpiPen Jr. Shiv's body creates its own set of dynamics: as a kid who was adopted, his body does not necessarily make sense in context, the way it might if his biological parents were standing next to him. I worry about him hearing the word "big" associated with him over and over again, worry that it will make him self-conscious or that others will judge him by his size, especially as a black male. We routinely fend off inquiries about his future sports career from strangers (though he's interested only in gymnastics and dance) and, at times, I have to remind myself that Shiv is in perfect health, even though others imply that his size must or will correlate to his health in a negative way. *He's a five-year-old with a tummy,* I want to tell people. *Chill the fuck out.*

Shiv's body presents logistic challenges, particularly as it relates to his clothing preferences. I thought of this as I read my friend Molly's essay about her partner's transition. Molly and I met when I was in graduate school, right around the same time she started dating Anne. I remember well the early blush of their love, their rightness for each other. Now Molly speaks of the difficulty in finding her partner clothes, of shopping in the boys' section, of learning which styles broaden shoulders or camouflage breasts. With Shiv, the challenge is related but on the other end of the spectrum; he is already wearing two to three sizes up for "boy" clothes, three to four sizes up for "girl" clothes. And the way he is shaped does not seem to match up with the shape of the hypothetical bodies kids' clothes are designed for—no one is taking my five-year-old's booty, tummy, or shoulders into consideration.

Having fought my own battles with ill-fitting clothes and felt shame at my body not corresponding to available styles, I work hard to be body positive with him, never implying shame or wrongness when clothes he tries on are tight. Everything I've read suggests that clothes and dress are a particularly fraught piece of the genderqueer puzzle, the quickest way for kids to gain or lose autonomy, a reminder that the world is not set up for them to feel good inside of their own skin. It's clear that Shiv's fixation on his outward appearance is about more than vanity; it is crucial to his identity. He's not the kind of person who can wear the same uniform each day or the kind of child who is content to have a parent pick their outfits. The anguish on his face when he can't get something to look the way he wants, the fact that the harshest punishment we've imposed to date (for unacceptable rudeness to his grandparents) was temporarily taking away his wigs and some of his dress-up clothes—that is information I can't ignore.

At this age, Shiv often passes for a girl, and it doesn't bother him to be mistaken for one. I'm amazed that he's read this way, even when wearing tennis shoes and with his natural, short hair showing. People see a dress and automatically decide "girl," even when he's displaying no other recognizable attributes of femaleness. Shiv is broad shouldered, sturdy: the type of body stereotypically read as masculine. I find it fascinating just how committed we are to the norms and categories we've created and what little room we have to imagine something else.

Truthfully, though, when people assume Shiv is a girl, it feels both like a relief and like we're getting away with something we won't be able to for long. Author and activist Janet Mock has written about how scary it can be for trans women of color to come out as trans, the risk of violence it brings. It was one thing to imagine Shiv growing into a large black man, but it's even scarier to imagine him as a large black trans woman or non-binary person.

I know we are approaching the limits of any kind of "pass" Shiv will get when it comes to being "just a kid" and breaking expectations related to gender. This is especially true because he is black; last week, I read a study showing that black kids get read as four and a half times older than they are compared with their white peers. Black boys, as they become men, are seen as dangerous, menacing. Darren Wilson testified that eighteen-year-old Michael Brown looked "like a demon" right before Wilson shot and killed Brown. Conversely, well-connected white men like Donald Trump's sons and his son-in-law, Jared Kushner, enjoy a kind of protracted childhood; they have the ear of the president of the United States and are granted unbelievable leniency when they make mistakes, even well into their thirties.

A few years ago, I bought an Elsa dress for Shiv at his request; around that same time, a Facebook post went viral in which a father explained why he had done the same for his son, railing against the norms and stereotypes that made it such an anomaly. The man and his son were white, as all of the people with wildly popular posts and tweets about gender-nonconforming children seem to be. When white kids defy gender norms, they are certainly vulnerable but still protected by their white privilege. Even a cursory look at statistics demonstrates the fact that violence against trans people disproportionately impacts trans people of color, specifically black trans women. And yet none of the resources I've found related to gender-creative parenting even acknowledge that race is a factor that will influence the public response and reaction my child receives, the enmeshed layers of complications and considerations. In fact, if you were to base your assumptions simply on the available children's books that show boys wearing dresses, you would think only white boys do it.

Try as I might, I seem unable to fight my impulse to find a reason for Shiv's unique choices. He's recently been insisting on wearing shirt hair at night, even if he hasn't worn it at all during the day. The other night, I asked him about it.

"Can you tell me why it matters to you to wear a shirt on your head at night?"

"Because I'm jealous of people who get to go to sleep with their long hair."

"Do you want to grow your hair out so it's long again?"

"No."

"You prefer the shirt?"

"Yeah, because it's so nice and I really, really, really like the way it looks!" Okay, then. That has to be good enough for me.

I think I feel compelled to understand in part because other people expect me to; they want me to explain Shiv's behavior to them, something I can't necessarily do. There's this little nagging voice that suggests, *If you were a better parent, you'd know the answer. If you knew him, you'd understand what this is about.* In this way, navigating the parent-child relationship is not unlike navigating a serious romantic relationship for the first time; in both instances, the desire to know and be known is necessarily balanced alongside the inability to fully understand another person. While I'm pretty sure that I know Shiv as well as anybody does, he is separate from me, and parts of him will always be mysterious, unknowable to me, even though I am his parent.

So too we are unknowable to ourselves; as much as Shiv has a strong self-conception, he's also just five years old. As a parent, I want to toe the line between honoring the self-knowledge he's asserting—not doubting or shrugging it off or acting as if he can't possibly know such things at such a young age—while also giving him space and time to explore, imagine, and unfold. I do not want him to feel pressured to identify with one camp or another, to "figure out" his identity in a way that makes other people comfortable. And I want to fight against the parental instinct to need Shiv to validate or mirror me in my personality, interests, or life choices.

Children of all kinds are often molded, whether intentionally or not, as developing representations of their parents: think of how much pride is implied when a parent claims that their child is a "mini me." This seems to be a natural instinct, one that I am sympathetic to and have experienced myself, but the problem is to what extent this projected mirroring perpetuates and reinforces cultural norms. As a teacher, I have a history of queer students finding their way to me as a first point of contact during the coming-out process. Subsequently their parents may seek me out as well, for advice and reassurance, and their concerns are always based in a sense of alarm that their child has surprised them and has turned out to be, in some fundamental way, different from them. How can their child know for sure that they're not straight? Is it possible they will change their minds? What are they supposed to do with the future scenes they've played out in their minds for years—proms, weddings, grandchildren—that now may never be realized?

Losing my father out of the blue taught me about the futility of assigning certainty to the future, so it has thus far been fairly easy not to speculate about Shiv's academic, romantic, or professional futures. But I never considered that I'd possibly need to let go of my attachment to Shiv's gender. Not until I sat down to write this paragraph did I recognize the irony; though not quite as blindsided as my parents were when I came out to them, I, too, have been surprised by an aspect of my child's identity that I hadn't seen coming.

So I work to make adjustments, small ones. I seek out certain images, spend time looking at them, interrogating my response. I fight my own impulse to register alarm when I see photos of the genderqueer and non-binary artists I follow on Instagram; their visibility makes apparent how black and white my own thinking still is. My task, then, is to retrain or interrupt my brain when I feel unsettled by a male body dressed in clothes that my mind codes as "female." To choose, instead, my intellectual response, which champions the way that these individuals are calling the whole construct of gender into question. I want my child to be able to play inside the world that they're creating, to love his body and wear whatever he wants, to call himself by whatever names and labels feel right to him.

I know that I will have some sadness if Shiv decides someday to fully transition, know that I have, on some level, built a part of my own identity around the idea of having a son. Lately, I find myself avoiding the term "my son" and replacing it with "my kid," so that I don't get overly attached to thinking about Shiv in a certain way, practicing for something I may or may not be called to do in the future. "Cotton is great because my kid gets so sweaty in the summer," I tell the salesclerk when she comments that a particular dress I'm buying for Shiv is cute.

I am encouraged that Shiv seems to feel free to experiment, to play around with language and expression. Last week, he asked permission to go visit at a neighbor's house, as he's done before; they have a son exactly two years younger than Shiv and a big backyard where the kids like to play. After getting dinner ready at our house, I walked down the street to retrieve Shiv. He begged for five more minutes, so I sat down on the patio with the other boy's mom. We chatted about the weather, her recent weekend trip. Then, out of the blue, she asked me, "Does Shiv have a sister?"

"What? I mean, no, he doesn't. He's an only child."

"Oh, hmm. When he came by today, he said, 'I'm not Shiv, I'm Shiv's sister.' I thought maybe he was wearing his sister's clothes." Shiv was wearing a polka-dotted dress and shirt hair, the first time he'd come over to this particular house dressed that way.

I immediately wondered if I should feel defensive, as I didn't know this mom well enough to know anything about her politics or beliefs. She didn't seem alarmed or upset, just maybe a bit curious. *Don't be preachy, just tell her the truth. Go easy, don't make it a big deal.*

"No, those are his clothes. He picked them out for himself. I think he's just exploring, kind of figuring out . . ."

"Who he is?" she finished my sentence for me. "Yeah, that makes sense."

This Is What a Family Looks Like

One thing I hate: car sticker families. You know the ones—little stick figure renderings of a mom, a dad, and a handful of kids, maybe the family dog or cat? Some are customized, with specific hairstyles and hobbies reflected in individual family members. There are thematically oriented sets, too: cowboys, pirates, elephants, owls, minions, aliens, superheroes, *Star Wars* characters; down here in Texas, I've started to see stickers in which each family member is represented by a different type of gun. "You've got your family, I've got mine," the copy reads. Delightful.

I'm not alone in my disdain for even the most innocuous seeming of these stickers; once they gained some popularity, I started to see new stickers that read, "Nobody cares about your car sticker family," with drawings of stick figures being eaten by a T. rex or chased by a storm trooper. These are perversely funny to me, sort of like the "My kid beat up your honor student" stickers that I found oddly compelling when I was younger, even though I myself was an honor student (one who would have been mortified had my parents labeled their cars accordingly). I disagree, though, with the statement that "nobody cares" about the car sticker families of others; of course we care. That's why they piss us off.

Car sticker families hit a cultural nerve. They feel like performative bragging, a demonstration that you have what everyone is supposed to want and strive to achieve: a heterosexual marriage, two or more kids (preferably one of each gender), a family pet, and a vehicle large enough to carry everyone around in. Placing a sticker on the back of your vehicle to show strangers what your family looks like strikes me as the ultimate demonstration of privilege. There are many who have avoided or seriously debated putting Black Lives Matter or Human Rights Campaign stickers on our cars for fear of vandalism or harassment.

But it's not only queer families or families of color who are unaccounted for in the proliferation of these stickers. Where are the stickers for blended families with stepkids and half-siblings? Or families where grandparents or uncles or aunts are the ones raising kids? Where is representation for the nannies and housekeepers and babysitters who perform essential supporting roles behind the scenes for, I suspect, many of the families driving the large SUVs sitting in private school carpool lines on which so many of these car stickers are placed?

I don't even know how I would *begin* to go about making a car sticker to represent my family. Where would I put Shiv's birth mother, who is undoubtedly and permanently included in how we think about "family," though we haven't spoken to her in years? Would we include Shiv's birth father, who was never interested in knowing his child? A depiction of my mother, who is an active and essential part of our life, but not my father, who's dead? What of Auntie Coco, whom we call "sister wife" but who lives in another state? Even if we could figure out whom to include, then there's the issue of what these stick figure people look like—the templates are crowded with girls wearing long hair and boys playing sports. And, of course, car sticker families are "color-blind" (that is, the default choice is white unless you seek out "full color" stickers, which are more expensive), so to accurately represent all of us would take some serious work.

The truth is that I would never bother to order a car sticker family and place it on my car, even if it were cheap, convenient, and uncomplicated. I don't understand the compulsion to do so, which is why I'm both fascinated and revolted by the sight of them. Ultimately, they are just annoying, like the voice of a singer you dislike but can't put your finger on why. Here, though, I suspect that I *do* know why: jealousy. I'm irked every time I see a car sticker family because anyone who puts one up has something I don't; there is no risk in showing their family to the world.

For my family, how we are perceived by others can be an adventure full of mistakes, questions, incorrect terminology, raised eyebrows, puzzled looks, or warm smiles. It's a grab bag: we never know what we're going to get. Often—especially when we're engaged in mundane or routine tasks, like going to the grocery store or the library, places we've been dozens of times—I don't think, worry, or wonder about any of these dynamics. But whenever we're going somewhere new, or one of us is coming along for the first time, I go on alert, monitoring the body language and behavior of the people around us, observing them observe us. Watching them try to do the math: Who goes with whom?

Shiv's been taking gymnastics this summer, at his own request, once a week for an hour. I drove him the first few times, reporting back to Jill how fun it was to watch him on the bar, on the beam, so she came along to see for herself. The class is a bit of a drive from our house, into the older part of town, which is much more politically conservative and demographically homogeneous. Drive twenty minutes from the natural foods grocery store by our house and you enter neighborhoods with large parcels of land, horses, and riding lawn mowers. A small distance can make a world of difference.

Which is why I was wary when I noticed one of the other gymnastics parents noticing us. She was white, about my age, with a daughter in Shiv's class and a younger son sitting with her. I'd seen her before, but now she was giving me and Jill the side-eye, refusing to meet my eyes or smile when I turned her way. Had she thought I was Shiv's biological mom, assumed my husband was black? Then I noticed her shirt—branded with the stylized American flag with a single blue line that's become emblematic of the Police Lives Matter movement. Then I realized that Jill and I were sitting next to the only other people of color in the space, a dad whose daughter was trying out class for the first time and two older girls who'd be doing their trial classes later. Was I imagining hostility from this mom, or was she genuinely sending it our way?

The sensation of being watched is almost palpable, though it's not always hostile; sometimes it's a gentle, friendly curiosity, while other times judgment, disapproval, or puzzlement come through clear as day. The response to my family is like a radio frequency—always there if I tune in to it. Is it the fact that we're two women with a child? Is it the fact that we're an interracial couple, a mixed-race family? Is it the fact that our child, whose body is male and large, often opts to wear clothes traditionally gendered as "girl"? Or is it all of these things?

Jill and I spend our lives tuned in to this frequency, to the point that we take for granted that others don't. I grew up watching people watch my family, because in Memphis we stood out: my father and I, dark skinned but not identifiably black, and my mom, much fairer skinned in a way people found harder to place. The lived experience of being watched and puzzled over time and time again becomes visceral, to the point that it can feel useless to try to convince your (white) friends that such watching and puzzling actually exists. Jill had certainly experienced it before Shiv, as a gay woman, but it's been interesting to watch her discover the level of scrutiny and spectatorship that adding Shiv to our family has brought. And perhaps not surprising, she has an easier time convincing other white people that what we experience isn't just our imagination.

Sometimes, our loved ones live into our family's experiences, building visceral, firsthand knowledge of what we regularly negotiate. A few summers ago, we were invited to spend the weekend at our friend's family lake house in Arkansas, a few hours' drive from Memphis. Driving behind our friends in a caravan, we followed them into the parking lot of a diner in what seemed like the middle of nowhere. "We always stop here for milkshakes on the way to the lake—the kids love it," they'd told us. Shiv, being a milkshake fan, was excited, and we thought nothing of it until we walked into the place. Jill and I immediately exchanged a look—this diner might have been a favorite of our friends, a white heterosexual couple with two biological kids—but we weren't optimistic that it would be a welcoming place for us, a two-mom, three-color family.

And we were right. No one was outwardly rude, but no one tried to hide their stares either. Shiv and I were the only people of color in sight, and his calling me "Mama" eliminated the possibility that he might be our friends' adopted child. Thankfully, our friends caught on immediately, assuming an upbeat and cheerful posture out of instinct, all of us trying to navigate the situation without speaking about it out loud. I sent Jill up to order food with my friend's husband, while she and I sat with the kids, working to keep a happy face on for the kids while futilely attempting to keep a low profile. I was hyperconscious of Shiv's behavior, not wanting to give anyone in that place an excuse to justify an existing opinion about black boys or two-mom families. My inner good southern girl prompted me to smile at a few of the people I caught staring, who pointedly did not smile back. We all ate quickly and made sure our kids did an excellent cleanup job, breathing a sigh of relief and raising eyebrows at one another as we walked out the door.

Unlike so many other awkward experiences I've lived through, this one resulted in a thoughtful and honest conversation between us and our friends, which is, of course, the best-case scenario, dependent on our friends' true open-mindedness and humility. More often, we find that even the most self-proclaimed "progressive" acquaintances and co-workers lack the willingness to align their actions with their beliefs, particularly when the result is an inconvenience to them.

Which brings me to the question of visibility, and what visibility can and cannot accomplish. Take social media: Jill and I have never been shy or reticent about posting pictures of Shiv; that's just not our way. We have both blogged in the past, sometimes sharing deeply personal news—I wrote about experiencing anxiety and seeking counseling after Shiv was born; Jill wrote about quitting her academic job as well as her experience with cancer. So it felt natural for us to share about our adoption journey and to celebrate Shiv's arrival and subsequent milestones. Pretty quickly, we realized that sharing news about our family was not always as simple as it might be for others. Most minorities know what it feels like to be seen as the representative for their respective group, a burden that can be, to put it mildly, tiresome. But when you combine all the factors at play in our family, that unwitting representation is amplified. For many of the people in our lives, the only family they know like ours is us. Maybe they know another two-mom family, but not a two-mom family who adopted. Or maybe they know a family who also adopted transracially, but the parents are straight. Or maybe they know two moms who adopted a black child, but both of the moms are white. We are often looked to for our responses: after a shooting, after an election, after we post an article about racial inequality. We are the unwitting experts, or, more accurately, the only point of contact, for so many of the people in our lives.

Sometimes I find this annoying, like *Can't y'all diversify your friend groups?* But then I figure I have a choice: if I'm going to post anyway, I might as well try to be cognizant of the impact my posts can have. I intentionally explain why we use the term "place for adoption" instead of "give up for adoption," because the former acknowledges Shiv's birth mother's participation in the process. Maybe doing so will cause someone I know to think about adoption differently, to consider a new narrative.

But posts on social media are no silver bullet for understanding— this kind of visibility works only when people are either already invested in us or otherwise open to changing their thinking. And I worry sometimes that people will think they get a pass on the political issues that are inherently personal for our family, that they can "like" our photos and videos without doing any intellectual digging. Still, I think about the impact that images have had on me; I recently started following a handful of trans and genderqueer artists on Instagram, and seeing their selfies each day causes me to reconsider the narratives running in my head, my default feelings about beauty and "passing" and what it means to perform gender. This buoys my confidence in the choice Jill and I have made to post photos of Shiv regardless of the outfit he's wearing at the time, which often means dresses, skirts, and/or wigs. It's not that we don't think about the fact that we might raise eyebrows or draw ire; it's that we don't let that stop us.

We have gotten only a little flak and pushback, namely one hostile text message from a family friend my mom's age, who later apologized; most people either don't object or manage to keep their objections to themselves. But even the smallest hint of hostility triggers in me a realization of how primed I am to fight back against the notion that we're somehow reinforcing the idea that two women shouldn't be parents, especially not of a boy.

I want things to go off without a hitch, afraid that every hitch we *do* encounter is just further fuel for the fire stoked by those who see us as perversions of a proper family. This feels akin to my parents' exhortations to perform as well as I possibly could in school, in order to disprove anyone who might be tempted to attribute my success to some kind of brown girl sympathy vote. I resented having to account for the opinions of others, but it felt perversely satisfying to think that my performance in school proved people wrong. What I didn't realize then was that this approach still meant living according to someone else's standards.

I know that people are going to look at Shiv's gender fluidity and say, *Well, that's what you get for letting two moms parent,* which makes me bitterly angry because I know that Jill and I are excellent, thoughtful parents. Because I know that "the right way" to parent, according to those same people, is the unquestioned, uninterrogated way of doing things, a way that has hurt and constrained so many people like my son. Maggie Nelson refers to "the eagerness of the world to throw piles of shit on those of us who want to savage or simply cannot help but savage the norms that so desperately need savaging." This is why my son in a dress with his two moms is so threatening, and also why he's so essential. Those of us who have been screwed by the traditional way may well prove indispensable in the work of creating more space for everyone.

About a year ago, I received an e-mail from the mom of one of Shiv's classmates—she wrote to RSVP for her daughter to attend Shiv's fourth birthday party. At the end, she tacked on this coda:

> I thought you would like this story. I asked K what she
> liked most about school this week. She, as usual, said
> she liked playing with her friends. And then she told me
> that she and A and Shiv were playing and she and A were
> the mommies and Shiv was the daughter and he took
> good care of the cat and dog. I didn't get any more
> details, but she was quite pleased with how the household
> was running. :-)
>   Your sweet family is a blessing to us.

This little girl has heterosexual parents, like the rest of Shiv's classmates, and this story from her mom puts me in mind of an assertion from Mahzarin Banaji, one of the Harvard University professors who developed the Implicit Association Test. Banaji talks about the power of the images we encounter, even something as simple as a photograph on a screen saver that we passively observe. What we see expands the scope of what we are able to imagine—"there is a point at which this brain is not just elastic in moving to what is being suggested, but that it may be plastic in that it can be reset into a new mold."

Hearing this, I think of my own mind, still molded a certain way despite my own experiences. A few years ago, a friend asked if she could bring along some out-of-town visitors to my family's annual tree-trimming celebration. "They're actually thinking about adopting, so I bet they'd love to talk to you, if you don't mind." I didn't mind and said I'd look forward to meeting them. When they arrived, I did a double take and had to cover up my surprise that the extra guests, who I'd assumed to be a straight couple, turned out to be two women. I'm so used to people adding on these markers of identity—"my black friend," "my gay uncle"—unthinkingly, whether they're necessary, that it threw me when my friend didn't. It wasn't essential for me to know that her friends were two women; I was inviting them into my home, not picking them up from the airport. They are her friends, not her "lesbian friends." This small omission confers so much dignity. I find it incredibly refreshing.

Same thing when three kids—two female and one male—decide to play-pretend family and imagine themselves as two moms with one daughter. Think of the freedom that comes with that expansiveness, what it would have made possible for so many of us to grow up with that narrative, how much shame it might have erased: the way it presses the reset button on "normal."

When Shiv was about three years old, he became interested in babies. Many of his friends had recently acquired siblings, and several of my friends were having their first children, so he was spending a lot of time around newborns and infants. This resulted in his first waves of jealousy—I love to hold babies, which was hard for him—as well as asking what he had been like as a baby. He invented "the baby game," in which he and I took turns being the mama or the baby, pantomiming crying, feeding, shushing, and rocking to sleep. Then, one day, while driving to the gym, he asked me the inevitable question: "Mama, how you make a baby?"

The ensuing conversation, with a little fumbling on my part, led to the purchase of a book, *What Makes a Baby,* that helpfully discusses the component parts of baby creation (sperm, egg, uterus) without going into the details regarding mechanics; I'm sure we'll get there soon enough. Instead, the colorfully illustrated book discusses how some bodies have sperm, and how some bodies have eggs, and that you need both to make a baby. You also need a place for the baby to grow—a uterus—and then, in that silly way of children's books, the book explains that even though the word "uterus" has the sounds "you" and "us" in it, only some bodies have a uterus. But the uterus is always in the same place in every body, the squishy part below the belly button.

The first time we read Shiv this book, he pointed to the spot below his belly button and asked eagerly, "Is this where my uterus is?"

"Oh, buddy," I said, stealing a look across the bed at Jill, "your body doesn't have a uterus." I figured he might be bummed to hear this, but I was wrong. He was *devastated.*

"I wanna have a uterus! I wanna grow a baby in my body!"

While Jill tried to console him with the fact that she, too, does not have a uterus (the result of a hysterectomy to treat uterine fibroids), I thought about how legitimate it was for him to be bereft. I hold sympathy for women whose infertility precludes them from conceiving and carrying a child, but I had never considered that boys or men might experience grief or disappointment over their biological inability to participate in pregnancy and childbirth. It must kind of suck to realize that you've been opted out of that prospect from the start.

When I relayed this story to a male friend, about twenty years older than me, his response to Shiv's reaction was "Yeah, that feeling got socialized out of the rest of us."

Shiv's mental flexibility around the way family works is due in large part to his own story, which he's always known. We have spoken about his adoption since he was born, never wishing to keep it from him or to pretend our family came into being in any other way. Trying to take his lead, we answer questions when they come up, not withholding or lying, while at the same time trying to gauge what makes sense to share in the moment. This year, when Facebook reminded me that June 27 marks the day we matched with Shiv's birth mother in 2012, I thought the occasion merited a dinner table acknowledgment and toast. (I am kind of a sucker for birthdays, anniversaries, and celebrations, and Shiv is like me in this regard, insistent that we say both "Amen"—his word for grace—and "Cheers" at every meal. We, the adults, often forget to hold hands and bow our heads before eating; he reminds us every time.)

"Hey, bud," I said, sitting down next to him at the table. "You know what today is?" He shook his head no.

"Five years ago today, Gigi and I got the best email ever—an email telling us that there was a birth mom who wanted to meet us! And you know who was growing in her tummy?"

"Me!" he responded jubilantly.

"That's right, it was you. Just a few days later, we had lunch with Mama D and met her for the first time."

"And we met you then, too," Jill added. "Because you were growing inside of her. And we were so happy and excited and nervous. It was very special." She reached over to squeeze his arm, which he wiggled in response, grinning.

Then his face fell. "I wish I could see her now," he said, referring to his birth mother. Mama D checked in with us via text fairly regularly during the first year of Shiv's life, but we haven't heard from her since his first birthday.

"I know you do, sweetheart," I said. "I can understand why that makes you feel sad. I'm sorry it's not possible to see her right now. We do have pictures of her, though. Would you like to look at them?"

He nodded yes. I went into the living room to grab his baby book, bringing it to the table and pointing to the pictures we have of Mama D—one sitting with Jill and me in the waiting area at a doctor's appointment and several in the hospital, holding Shiv after he was born. On her face, you can see the complication of the moment: deep love and wonder, with pain and a touch of uncertainty.

"See how she's holding you?" Jill pointed to the page. "She loved you so much. She was very brave."

Everyone's adoption story is different: Closed adoptions that leave adoptees with a deep longing to find their birth families and closed adoptions that leave adoptees with absolutely no desire to find their birth families. Partially open adoptions, like ours, where birth mother and/or birth parents become integrated into the adoptee's life and are sometimes known for who they are, sometimes introduced as an aunt or a cousin. Some families take vacations with their children's birth mothers; others never even meet them in person. And while I think I was prepared, at least intellectually, to experience Shiv's sadness and sense of loss related to Mama D, it took me by surprise when he seemed to focus more on his birth father.

Shiv's greatest source of grief in his young life has been about "not having a daddy." While his birth mother is specific, a person

Jill and I knew and can share details about, a woman whose picture he can see with his own eyes, his birth father is an unknown, someone about whom we know little, and none of it very good. And Shiv's longing seems to go beyond one specific person; it's not just his birth father—it's having a father in general. "I wish I had a daddy," he has said more than once. Almost everyone he knows, including both of his moms, has a daddy. Culturally, everything geared toward young children—school, books, TV shows—talks about "mommies and daddies."

I was prepared for our family structure to give him some trouble, for it to be difficult once he realized that his family was not exactly the same as everyone else's. But his position is not either/or; it's both/and. He routinely shouts, "I love my two moms!" or, "I have the best parents!" as he pulls the three of us into a group hug. He doesn't seem to be wishing us away—at least not yet!—but rather to be longing for something, or someone, that isn't here. All children tend to focus on what others have and what they don't; they're comparative by nature, whether it's housing, clothes, toys, or food that they're focused on. My years of teaching have made it clear that there is no such thing as a child who isn't envious of what someone else has, but still, I am hypersensitive to any indication from Shiv that his family structure is a disappointment.

Over Memorial Day weekend in 2017, our friends Dave and Burke had their first baby—a boy, Hugo. Dave is one of my closest friends, and the first time I met Burke, Shiv was only ten days old, which means Shiv has known "Uncle Dave" and "Aunt Burke" his whole life. On the day Hugo was born, I showed Shiv the video that Dave had sent me from the hospital room: Hugo, brand-new and wiggling on the baby scale, gripping one of Dave's fingers with a tiny hand.

"You looked like that when you came out, too, bud," I said. "Gigi and I were right there."

"Did I hold your finger like that?"

"You held Gigi's finger. She talked to you like Uncle Dave was talking to Hugo."

Minutes later, driving home in the car, we pulled up alongside a motorcycle—a big Harley with a large black man in the seat, probably about ten years older than me. He caught Shiv's attention, because motorcycles always do, and must have sparked a series of associated thoughts. As the motorcycle sped away, Shiv asked, "Was my birth father in the room when I was born?"

"No, sweetheart, he wasn't. We never met him."

"Why not?" A difficult question to answer with honesty, without breaking your child's heart.

"Well . . . he and your birth mother, they weren't really in a relationship together. By the time you were born, they weren't part of each other's lives."

"Where is he now?"

"I don't know, sweetie."

"But how I can communicate with him?" The combination of his correct use of a "big kid" word and the attendant desperation in his voice was devastating.

"I don't know, buddy. It's not something that's possible, at least not right now. I'm so sorry. I know you wish you could." Pause. "What would you tell him if you could talk to him?"

"That I want him to come pick me up from school sometime. That I want to see him."

"Maybe we could write a letter to him. You can tell me what words to write and then you can decorate it. Even though we can't send it, it might feel good to put your feelings down. I still do that with Nanaji, you know."

Nanaji means "mother's father" in Hindi and is the name Shiv uses for my dad, who has been dead for over a decade; he is only "Nanaji" in the abstract. I wrestled with grief for many years before Shiv came along, but his arrival complicated that grief, adding another layer to it. Missing my father is one thing; knowing that my son will never have the opportunity to know his grandfather is another.

Everything I've learned about grieving—that there's no "fixing it," that grief does not necessarily equal "something's wrong"—is more difficult to hold on to when it's Shiv who's experiencing the grief. As a parent, I find it so tempting to rush in and say, *Buddy! Having two moms is okay! Lots of your friends are jealous of your two moms! Sometimes dads aren't all they're cracked up to be!* But it's crucial, I know, to let him experience the sense of loss and feel the sadness. I think of the frustration I felt every time someone tried to manage or minimize my own hurt, and I want so desperately not to do that to him.

In the first few years after my dad died, I learned to be careful about expressing my grief in front of my mother. My sense of loss and devastation was almost pathologically triggering for her; she simply couldn't be with it. Though she herself was reeling from the same loss, being reminded that *I* was suffering was almost more painful for her. I learned to work around this, but it irked me that I had to. Now I feel like I understand.

It's humbling to think that my child, my own family, the true and full story of how we came to be and what we are, challenges and expands my notion of what family looks like. Shiv can love having two moms and also wish he had a dad. We can be wonderful parents and Shiv can also long for his birth mother. Our story can be messy and complicated while still being good.

July 2 is a big day in my house: not only is it my mom's birthday but it's also the day that Jill and I got married. We did this on purpose; we were eager to get married as quickly as we could following the *Obergefell* Supreme Court decision in 2015, and my mom's birthday was six days later. Since that first year, we've established the tradition of getting a babysitter and going out to dinner the three of us, sans Shiv, at a restaurant we all love but can't afford to go to except once a year. I always volunteer to drive, so that we can get my mom a little bit drunk. Generally, my mom is funny and sassy and passionately opinionated, and she becomes only more so with a glass of sangria followed by a shared bottle of wine.

The first year, the folks sitting at the table next to us began conspicuously pointing and looking over at us halfway through our meal.

"What is their deal?" Jill asked.

"They're trying to figure us out," I responded.

"What, they've never seen three women together?" My mom giggled.

As a crew, we don't immediately make sense—we are not three women people are accustomed to seeing together, not part of the conventional family narratives. I wonder how many people would guess the true nature of our group: mother, daughter, daughter-in-law. And I wonder whether it matters.

Etymologically speaking, the word "mistaken" is related to "misapprehension"; "apprehend" comes from the Latin that means "to grab hold of, grasp." To be a new kind of family is to feel like people are working hard to grab hold of us, but that they cannot, at least not at first glance. We're slippery fish.

The summer that Shiv mastered a balance bike, we spent many evenings on the neighborhood golf course path, taking advantage of the slightly cooler temps afforded by dusk. One night, a woman whose backyard faced the golf course overheard Shiv call me "Mama" and looked at me puzzled, then accusing.

"I thought *she* was his mom." She pointed at Jill, who was walking a few paces behind. Turns out that Jill and Shiv had interacted with this woman a few days prior, without me there. I bet this woman thought she was dealing with a heterosexual white woman with a white husband who (so magnanimously and generously!) had adopted a black child; I was an unwelcome interruption in that narrative. Even though she was the one who didn't seem to know what to do with me, I still managed to feel embarrassed. This is a scenario I recognize from childhood, when people would guess at my ethnicity or assume that my mother was not my mother because she is much lighter skinned than me. Inevitably, I wound up feeling like I had done something wrong, all because my family did not make sense to someone else.

Shiv, thankfully, seems to feel no such embarrassment. "I have two moms," he told the golf course woman. "A Mama and a Gigi." And that was that.

Jill chose the name "Gigi" when Shiv was born, to avoid Mom/Mommy/Mama confusion and because she liked that it sounded like Jill. Though occasionally people mistake it for a grandmother name, overall it has served her and Shiv well. Whereas I was pretty attached to the prospect of responding to the title of "Mama," Jill felt some reticence about buying into everything that comes with conventional notions of #momlife. She isn't a lot of things that people expect moms to be, has never experienced herself as maternal or felt the tick of a biological clock. But she is the one who felt morally compelled by the prospect of adoption, the one who led us as a family to adoption. And as Shiv's Gigi, Jill has proved to be a source of refuge, patient teacher, beloved playmate, and thoughtful co-parent.

After adopting, Jill and I volunteered to place our contact information on a list of references that our agency could provide to prospective families, specifically other LGBTQ folks. One woman sticks out in my mind, not for the dozens of questions she had about the adoption process (those I was prepared for) but rather for asking, rather abruptly, "Which one of you is the 'daddy'?" Puzzled, I took longer than the polite amount of time to craft a response.

"Well . . . neither. We, um, don't think about our family in those terms."

"Oh, well. I just assumed that one of you would be. It's very important to my wife to be the daddy when we have kids." Advocates for and reinforcement of norms can come from seemingly unlikely sources.

When we struggle to talk about something, it reveals a gap in our collective thinking. In this way, "Gigi" creates something new, and not just for our family; Shiv's teachers and friends all know that Jill is his Gigi and refer to her accordingly. Philosopher Bertrand Russell asserted that "language serves not only to express thought but to make possible thoughts which could not exist without it." Whenever there is a push for new terminology, or more sensitivity in speech, a sector of the public will cry foul, allege "political correctness," imply that such an emphasis on speech is soft or silly or otherwise pointless. I agree that to only change speech is not enough, but what's clear to me is that this resistance to changing language is a resistance to being asked to do any kind of work. When the default position is tailored to fit you, being asked to give something up feels like an affront, an injustice. Don't take away my flag, my monument, my team mascot, my slur.

But sometimes damage has to be done, the kind of destruction that makes way for something new. And there is real power in invading or interrupting conventional spaces. You show up where you aren't expected and you manage to make room for yourself, make yourself comfortable, make yourself right at home. You test the limits of others' self-proclaimed open-mindedness, call them out, fighting against the instinct to be gracious and agreeable, as you were raised: to not make a fuss.

To retrain ourselves to speak differently is a way of indicating that we care enough to be more precise, to make space for others who are different. Yes, it requires more of me to use the pronouns "they" and "them" when requested, requires me to retrain my brain and stumble around as I do, but is that so hard? Is that not effort I am willing to expend to be in a relationship, to become better, more thoughtful, to do less damage? To ask what matters to others, and to then demonstrate a willingness to take on the answer as our own concern, is a form of generosity I believe we can all cultivate.

Afterword to the Paperback Edition

I am standing next to Jill inside the main lodge at a campsite called Whispering Pines, about three-quarters of the way up Mount Lemmon, northeast of Tucson, Arizona. We drove here earlier today from our house in Phoenix so that Shiv could attend Camp Born This Way, a weekend for transgender and gender-queer kids and their families. It's our first time attending, and we weren't quite sure what to expect, but so far it feels a lot like good ole summer camp—hikes and s'mores and little blue plastic trays for the mess hall—only with the notable addition of make-your-own pronoun badges and a total lack of gender designations for anything. All of the fun, none of the conformity.

Case in point: the dance party taking place in the lodge at this very moment. It's like every awkward dance party I endured in my youth: too brightly lit, linoleum floors, metal-legged chairs pushed to the side to clear a dance floor, and orange coolers filled with Gatorade and water as refreshments. But somehow, here the air is electric. The music is good—I shouldn't make generalizations about queer parties, but one that feels safe to make is that we tend to be pretty on point when it comes to music—and everyone is actually dancing. There's a group of teenagers assembled in a circle, as they do, the same posse who spent most of the day playing Dungeons & Dragons, laughing and joking and breaking it down. There are the little ones, dressed in their dance party finest, which has been embellished during unsupervised time at the free-for-all makeup table that was set out this afternoon on the porch, wiggling and giggling with joy, twirling and hopping with abandon. They are watched by the architects of this space, the trans and genderqueer adults who volunteer to plan and coordinate this weekend in order to give kids like mine a kind of refuge, something these adults themselves did not have growing up. Then there are the parents, who come from multiple demographic categories and would likely have never crossed paths were it not for the common denominator of our children. As some of the only queer women here, Jill and I have had a kind of a leg up in recognizing a sliver of our child's experience; we know what it means not to fit, how painful it is to have to fight for the ability to live and express yourself in an authentic way. Still, all of the parents in this space, regardless of their own identifications, have chosen to honor their children's knowledge about themselves; hearing stories from some of these parents has left me astonished at the degree to which these kids know the truth about themselves and have managed to articulate and advocate for that truth. The fact that many of these parents have traveled a long way in their own views about gender in recent years is an astonishing rebuke to the notion that trans identities are "planted" in children by adults with an agenda.

The opening notes of "Dancing Queen" blare out, because of course, have you even had a dance party if you haven't played ABBA? I pull Jill out to the middle of the dance floor, grinning. It is so powerful to watch these young people move freely inside this space, wearing the clothes and makeup they've chosen, holding hands with one another if they wish, unselfconscious and unafraid. In so much of the world, they would be unsafe doing what they're doing right now. But for this moment, they get to be exactly who they are, instead of trying to make themselves fit or managing the consequences that might come if they don't. There is no worrying or hiding or strategizing; here, they simply get to dance.

I reach out to put my hand on Jill's shoulder so that I can speak directly into her ear: "This is the weirdest, queerest, and absolute best dance party I have ever been to in my entire life."

"I know," she says as she smiles back. "Me too."

When I submitted the final edits for *Brown White Black* in August 2017, our family was living in Houston and Shiv had just turned five. At that point, it was clear to Jill and I that we had a child who did not conform to traditional gender norms; Shiv was spending more and more time in dresses, wearing wigs, and talking about princesses and female superheroes. But Shiv also loved to wrestle/play-fight, relished getting dirty, and sometimes chose to wear clothes conventionally gendered as "male." Because of this, we had started using language like "our kid" instead of "our son," but we still referred to Shiv using male pronouns, because Shiv had registered no objections otherwise. We knew it was likely this would change down the line, but it seemed counterproductive to speculate or try to guess how older Shiv might identify: Genderqueer? Agender? Transgender? Non-binary? Our approach all along has been to follow Shiv's lead, providing resources and support without pushing. We try not to plan or imagine too many specifics about our child's future, gender related or otherwise.

By the time *Brown White Black* came out into the world in February 2019, our family had moved a thousand miles away to

Phoenix, and Shiv had begun using female pronouns, living life as a girl at school, home, dance class, etc. Though we hadn't planned it this way, the move provided Shiv with the perfect opportunity to start fresh.

We shared the news with our friends and family back in Houston and scattered elsewhere around the country. In lieu of a grand announcement, we started switching the pronouns we used to refer to Shiv on social media—given that we'd been posting pictures of her in dresses and wigs for a couple of years by that point, no one seemed all that surprised. But they did have questions. (People always have questions.)

"Does it feel different, now that Shiv's a girl? Has it been hard? What's changed?"

In truth, it's as if everything has changed and as if nothing has changed, all at once. Shiv is a remarkably consistent human, someone who knows what she wants and isn't afraid to articulate or ask for it. She is now, as she was at the time I wrote the book, a wildly extroverted, theatrical, creative, effusive, and tenacious child. She instigates family dance parties, obsesses over her hair, loves books, and is extravagant with her affection. All of those things were true before, too.

But it's not only pronouns and language that have changed—words are how we create our world, and the world that Shiv lives in now is a world that's been constructed by language that feels right to her, for her. It was during our time at Camp Born This Way that Shiv claimed the term "trans" for herself, identifying that way for the first time. With that language comes new territory and new sets of considerations to navigate: travel documents, medical care, what it means to parent someone who identifies as "female" in American society. How do we balance Shiv's entitlement to privacy with our desire for her not to feel ashamed of who she is?

How do we celebrate her identity inside our family while also preparing her for the world as it is?

To a certain extent, we've used many of the same strategies we've employed from the beginning—helping her unwrap the many layers of her self by using whatever means we can to ensure that she spends the majority of her time in supportive spaces and environments. The day before I interviewed for my job in Phoenix, I toured the school where Shiv now attends, needing to confirm that it would be a good fit before I could say yes or no to my job offer; I left a completed application and deposit behind at the school before even signing an employment contract.

At the same time, we are careful not to shield Shiv from the truth of the world "out there"—we are her advocates now, but she has to learn to advocate for herself when we're not around. So we do our best to model for her, just as we do when showing her a cooking or gardening technique, except in this case we're explaining what it means to "pass" or how to enlist the help of an ally. Sometimes it's demoralizing to feel like our kid already has so much on her plate, and that it's only going to get more complicated for her as she gets older. But our wish that it were otherwise doesn't ultimately serve her.

I'm buoyed by the fact that Shiv seems to have solid footing inside the values and principles we've set forth as a family, to the extent that when she encounters other messaging—which has already happened and will certainly continue to—she doesn't internalize it. She knows her truth. And watching her flourish inside that truth has brought me and Jill great joy, as well as confirming for us that letting Shiv lead the way was the right choice.

A Q&A with the Author

What was one central goal you wanted to accomplish by writing this book (could also be goals, if you'd prefer that)?

I try not to write with the end in mind; if I do, I find that my writing becomes too didactic and predictable, not something that anyone would want to read. Instead, I approach my work through a lens of exploration—I write to discover what I think about a particular topic, question, or idea. With this book, I knew that I wanted to write about my family, that there were a few stories or experiences that stuck in my mind, but I wasn't sure why they were significant to me and what, if anything, they signified more broadly. I used the book as a framework to read and think about my own sense of identity and how getting married and becoming a parent—specifically the non-black parent of a black child—had shifted my sense of who I was, as well as my thinking about larger concepts like family. My ultimate hope is that I am able to be honest with myself first, such that readers can connect with that honesty and take from it whatever they find valuable or meaningful in their own lives.

Have you and Jill changed at all since the book was published in terms of how you interact within your family or with those around you?

In many ways, the book solidified our approach to parenting and family, and, in that sense, it serves almost as a piece of family history from a particular portion of our life. We joke that, especially living in a new city, it's handy when people we're getting to know have read the book first, because we know that they're "on board" with certain things about how our family works, and it saves us from repeated explanations! At the same time, our work is ongoing; Jill and I are continually trying to examine and strengthen our thinking in response to what we see around us and what we see Shiv needing now, or potentially needing in the future. Shiv's gender identity has come more front and center in her self-conception at the same time that broader social questions about gender norms and transgender rights have proliferated. This has pushed both me and Jill into more of an activism and advocacy role, knowing that, for many of the people in our life, we are their most visible connection to the topic.

At the same time, I feel that the book is an important reminder to me that this work of self-examination and growth is a process; I want to remain humble and not fool myself into thinking that I haven't made missteps along the way. I am much more likely to judge others if I erase evidence of my own learning curve.

What was Shiv's reaction to the book and its reception? How did you explain writing the book and its contents to her?

I started writing the book when Shiv was two and a half and finished writing it around the time she turned five; for a while, her conception of "Mommy's book" was pretty vague, just a thing I did that meant she got to have lots of playdates with friends so I could write! Then, as we were preparing for the book to come out, she got pretty excited that her picture (our family picture) was on the back. She wanted to know if she was going to be "famous," probably because she thought that being famous meant getting to meet Beyoncé. Sadly, Mommy's book has proven a disappointment on that count.

Our more serious conversations about the book happened after it was published, at which time Shiv was six and a half, able to understand and appreciate much better what it meant that I had written a book about our family. She came with me to Houston for the book launch, not to go to the event (I am very cagey about doing anything that might smack of "parading her around" in front of an audience) but to visit with the good friends she misses. On the day after the launch, she and I went out to lunch, just the two of us, before getting on a plane to head back to Arizona. She asked a few questions about the event: if there were a lot of people there, if they had read my book or were going to read it. Then we had the following exchange:

"How does it feel for you, knowing that people are reading about us, about our family, about you?"

"It's a little weird."

"Why do you think I wanted to write about us, even though it is a little weird?"

"Because you want people to know what our family is about."

"Yeah, baby, that's exactly right."

"Well then you should write another book about us!"

Acknowledgments

The story of this project begins with two emails from two extraordinary women. The first is my dear friend, the brilliant writer Aisha Sabatini Sloan (if you haven't read *Dreaming of Ramadi in Detroit*, please do so immediately). Following up on a blog post I'd written about Shiv, Aisha wanted to know if I might have other stories to tell about race, adoption, and parenting; her belief in my voice led directly to my writing the first version of "Black Is the Color of My True Love's Hair," which was published online in *Guernica Magazine* in March 2015. That piece caught the eye of this story's second heroine, Anna deVries, whom I am now lucky enough to call my editor.

I must thank another editor, Lauren LeBlanc, who worked with me on "Black Is the Color." Her relentless integrity and exacting eye helped me refine my thinking about the stories that would eventually make up this project, and I am grateful for her energy and her friendship. Many thanks also to the staff at *Guernica*, who generously gave my writing a home, and the folks at the NPR *Code Switch* blog, who posted an excerpt from the piece one

Saturday morning, serving both as a tremendous vote of confidence and as a lesson to never read comments online.

My memories of writing this book are inextricably bound up in the structural changes and sacrifices that my family, both immediate and extended, made in order to create the time and space for me to do the work. I am forever grateful to Linda Draper and the staff at Blossom Heights for providing such a loving and affirming environment inside which Shiv could learn and thrive, allowing me to fully utilize my summers to work on this manuscript. A small bevy of babysitters and family friends welcomed Shiv for dozens of play dates and zoo trips, allowing me to sneak in writing time on weekends: Lauren Schoen, Bram Lowenstein, Hannah Plantowsky, Noah Pacht, Hannah Golub, the Goodman girls (Audrey and Rachel), Sophia Zulu, Uncle Jim and Aunt Julie, Silas and his moms, Ellie and her parents, and the Hudley crew—thank you, thank you, thank you.

There is no way to overstate the influence that my students have on me, generally and in connection to this project. Their willingness to take risks, to push themselves, to show up with vulnerability, to write with honesty, to accept criticism with grace—all of this has served to make me a better person, teacher, and writer. Thank you to my former work wife, Amanda Lucas, for modeling what lifelong learning looks like, and for bringing me chocolate when I really needed it. Deepest gratitude to Kristine Varney and Cara Henderson, silver linings in embodied human form, without whom I might not have made it through the most difficult school year of my life.

From the start, this book has had many cheerleaders who have turned what could have been a wholly solitary undertaking into a collective effort. Burke Butler, who asks the most insightful questions, and her husband, Dave Berry, one of my oldest friends,

brought a kitchen island's worth of take-out to celebrate the signing of my book contract, and regularly permitted me to snuggle
their sweet newborn, Hugo, when I needed a sanity break. Big
kisses to another snuggly newborn, Alice; her million-dollar-smile
big brother, Marcus; and her parents, Sacha and Maconda Abi-
nader, all of whom have been unfailingly supportive of me and
this project. I'll never forget Maconda asking, "What can we take
off of your plate?" when I was working up to a deadline—the self-
lessness with which she shows up for others is truly remarkable.
Rebecca Villarreal, who has walked with me through more major
life events than we bargained for when we met our freshman
year of college, listens to my hopes, fears, and anxieties during our
weekly phone date, and always knows what to say to make me feel
heard and understood. Katherine Bush and Shari Ray are talented
writers and master teachers who have offered me the gift of relating to me as a peer; they have demonstrated their love for and faith
in me for many years. David Waters has mentored and inspired me
since I was a sophomore in high school; Leanne Klinemann has
offered me support and encouragement in the most generous way.
Tim Mazurek and Sarah Searle are internet friends who became
real-life friends and both have made my life so much righter as
a result. Josh Foster has been my champion since we met in an
MFA workshop in Arizona and is the brother I always wanted,
as well as the uncle Shiv loves playing with the most.

Megan Batchelor is my Queen of Everything Good, the one
who resets my true north, makes me laugh, and restores my sanity
with just her smile. She is, famously, responsible for introducing
me and Jill, and for that alone I am indebted to her for life. Jen
Bauer-Conley is my sunshine, the woman who brought theater
back into my life and jump-started some of the most fulfilling
work of my teaching career, then became one of my best friends in

the process. Lue Bishop, aka Mama Lue, is a jackpot I managed to hit as a brand-new teacher; her mentorship of me and the way she consistently leads by example has changed me forever.

I would be remiss if I did not thank our family's wider village, the chosen family that has shown up for us for so many years and in so many ways: Greg Lopp and Sharon Stinson, Vicky Julian and Lois Kemp, Kym King, Bonnie Dayton, and Christian and Lisa Seger. Though far away, Marynelle Wilson, Phil Imus, Noa Gutow-Ellis, Emily White, Rachel Miller, and my "Arkansas group" aunties and uncles have lent their support and encouragement in ways that have made a true difference. I am indebted to the folks behind JustCity Memphis (www.justcity.org) for the incredible work that they do, and for allowing me to be a part of it. Special thanks to Josh Spickler for helping me understand the difference between wishful thinking and hope, and how to hold on to the latter. And my love and gratitude always to Lurene Kelley and Kerry Hayes for countless Spotify playlists and their honest, abiding friendship.

Maria Massie, thank you for taking a chance on me and for advocating for me each step of the way—every writer should be so lucky, but I know not all of us are. Anna deVries, you are essentially this book's midwife and I am regularly astounded by your patience, wide-ranging intelligence, and the deliberateness with which you take what you believe and translate that into the work you do. No doubt my life would be very different had you not arrived in it.

My beta readers—Jill Carroll, Courtney Rath, and Courtney Humphreys—are also three of the most important women in my life. They each gave many hours toward making this book more honest, more precise, and more thoughtful. Jill, your willingness to let me put our family's life on the page is fundamental to this book's existence, and your commitment to doing so with rigorous integrity has irrevocably changed the way I tell stories. Coco, your brain and your passion for justice have taught me so much; this book and I would be a mess without you. Court, your heart is unlike any other, and the way you speak truth has made not only our friendship but also my writing, stronger. I love all three of you more than I can say.

And then there were four: my father, my mother, my wife, and our child. Papa, I question so many things about how our lives would intersect were you still with us, but one thing of which I am certain is how proud you would be of this book. Amma, you are the rock at the center of the nuclear family I spent a long time thinking would never be possible. There's no way I can thank you for even a fraction of all you do, but your care and encouragement are just as powerful to me now as they were when I was a little girl. For every story you read me, each book you bought me, all the family dinners you cook with love, and the way you step in without hesitation to support me, Jill, and Shiv, I am grateful beyond measure. Jill, you have taught me so much about what it means to hustle, to make a dream real, and to show up for myself. You keep me honest, remind me of myself when I forget, and never once waver in your conviction that what I have to say is worthy. For keeping the plates spinning, for the thoughtfulness and joy you bring to co-parenting Shiv, for loving me so well—you are, and always will be, the best thing that ever happened to me. And, of course, Shiv, my treasure, you are the best thing that ever happened to *us*. I know that writing this book will likely bring some complication into your life, and that there may be times when you wish that I hadn't. My hope is that you will be able to understand why I believe sharing stories is so important, and that you will always know that being your mama is an honor I strive to be worthy of each day. I love you to the moon and back.